Readers Praise

EXTRAORDINARY DREAMS OF AN IRELAND TRAVELER

This is not a typical travel book, but also a wonderful photo book of the many attractions of Ireland. The author has put a lot of research into describing the places she visited. This is a book that you should carry with you in your travels. It is a true guide to a fun and successful vacation. I would rate the book 5-stars!

– Marty Wright, Napa, California

If anyone is contemplating a trip to Ireland, *Extraordinary Dreams of an Ireland Traveler* is a must. It is easy reading and is full of vivid descriptions of the "must see" places to help you plan your trip. I highly recommend it to anyone thinking of travel or even if you only want to experience the trip "second hand." Rosemary (Mamie) has done a marvelous job as a tour guide in book form!

— S. Allan Kane Jr., M.D., California

Waterford is one place described in this book that I had better not miss. The crystal factory tour was so much fun to see. Thank you for taking us every inch of the way through it. It was fun to see the process of how this expensive crystal was made. The photos made it much better than just reading about it.

— Patrick Snow, International Best Selling Author of *Creating Your Own Destiny* and *The Affluent Entrepreneur*

As someone who has visited Ireland, I can verify that Rosemary hits all the highlights and many "off the beaten path" points of interest that I missed. Her valuable advice on places to stay and attractions to see made me want to return to

the Emerald Isle to see what I missed the first time—in fact, the pictures made me homesick for the land of my ancestors.

— Tyler R. Tichelaar, Ph.D. and author of the award-winning *Narrow Lives* and *My Marquette*

Rosemary's book made Ireland come alive for me! I can't wait to go.

— Kate Phillips, www.TotalWealthCoaching.com

WOW! What an adventure. This is such exciting reading with adventures and history all in one. I enjoyed learning about the areas, but it felt nice not to feel as though I were in a history class! Learning about the Vikings was such an interesting story.

— Natalie Newport, author of *Ninja Nanny*

Loch Lein Country Manor - what a fabulous place in the country. Away from the city bustle and yet close to everything. A very romantic place and we loved the hosts. It was also close to Limerick where there is a lot to see. Thanks for the close up look!

— Nathan French, author of *My New Focus: It's Not A Secret*

What a story about the "Gift of Gab!" The height would be a bit scary especially when lying upside down. Not sure I want to do that but can't wait to see the others kiss the Blarney Stone.

— Randi Reed, International Flight Attendant

What fun that must have been playing with the hats at Blarney's! And I couldn't believe that you actually got back in business just three weeks after retirement, importing those designs into the states. That was some adventure! Keep us posted— Oh, and thanks for the special on woollens.

— H.C. (Joe) Raymond, author of *Embracing Change from the Inside Out*

Great human interest story about Blarney's and Aine. It was fun to read about the people there and their success stories especially when one of them reads much like Walt Disney's life. It was amazing to see how someone went from nothing to an empire.

— Frank Reed, author of *In God We Trust: Dollars and Sense*

EXTRAORDINARY DREAMS
of an
IRELAND TRAVELER

To: Elisabeth — The Sweetest Organizer a person could know. Enjoy the Journey! Rosemary "Mamie" Adkins 1-13-12

AVIVA
PUBLISHING

NEW YORK

ROSEMARY "MAMIE" ADKINS

Address all Inquiries to:

Rosemary (Mamie) Adkins

c/o Miss Mamie's Company, LLC

5912 Harlow Drive

Bremerton, WA 98312

360-377-9199

RosemaryAdkins@ExtraordinaryIreland.com

ISBN: 978-1-935586-53-1

Library of Congress #2011944560

First Printing: January 2012

Editor: Tyler Ticheelar

Cover Design & Interior Layout: Fusion Creative Works, ww.fusioncw.com

Please visit our website at:

www.ExtraordinaryIreland.com

Online ordering is available for Book and Some Products

Printed in the USA by JB Gray Printing

DEDICATION

This book is dedicated to my family and friends who have supported my dream of writing a book. I was discouraged as a child and told that it was uncouth for a young woman to be a writer, so now in my senior years, I appreciate the friends and family who supported my decision to try.

Cast and Crew from Bunratty Castle Medieval Banquet Dinner Show

I especially want to thank my husband, Douglas E. Adkins, for his patient love, support, and endless hours helping me with this book and sharing the journey with me.

Also special thanks to our daughter, Kecia Adkins Doke, who has always made us proud and for her support in telling me to follow my dreams. Thank you also to my son-in-law, Jonathan Doke, for his sensitive nature and patience. I love you both.

I have also been fortunate enough to have the support of friends who have proofread my work. I want to thank Vonnie Adkins, Herbert and Diane Hazen, John Hazen, Allan Kane, MD, Martha Wright, Bonnie McIntosh, Nancy Strawn, Cathy Lang, Kimberly Guance, and countless others from Ireland who put up with my errors, receiving multiple copies to proofread sent during my delusional phase when I thought I could work all night without making mistakes! Thank you all for believing in me! A big thank you to my mother-in-law for her undying support while I was planning this journey, writing my book, and realizing my dream. I also want to give thanks to God for inspiring me to be the best I can be and for giving me a new start in life.

Thank you to all our new friends across the seas for their help, patience, and informative help. Without you, there would be no story!

Special Thanks

MANY THANKS TO MY PARTNER, FRIEND, AND HUSBAND
DOUGLAS EARL ADKINS

My husband is the love of my life. He has been my partner for more than twenty years, so with that said, I want you to meet the man who in some ways is my co-author. We have traveled most journeys together and this one was no different. He put up with all the "stuff" a writer's spouse or partner puts up with  while I wrote my book. He was ignored for hours, or days, as my mind worked faster than my fingers. And he, like other writers' partners, was there to put me back together every time I "hit the wall!" So, how could I not call him my co-writer! He is my co-pilot and just as important to the writing process as a co-pilot is to an international flight.

This book, or writing a book, has been my dream, not his, yet he supports my efforts and applauds my persistence to finish.

Dear, you are my partner in every way. Thank you for all that you are. I love you dearly and certainly give you credit for being my co-author!

Above all, I dedicate this book to you.

KECIA ADKINS DOKE
OUR FABULOUS DAUGHTER

Our daughter deserves many thanks because she has supported my dreams for years. Her encouragement and her own achievements have given me the courage to write this book about Ireland. She inspired me to be the best mother possible; we love her so much and we are proud of who she is.

I'm sure she must have been frustrated as I sent her my chapters in duplicate. However, she never complained, but sent me messages of praise and suggestions when she found areas that needed work. I remember when she was just a small child how she would ask me to tell her stories and later encouraged me to write about my life when I would talk about my dreams to do so. Because I have written this book, I feel the other book is now possible.

Thank you for being the best daughter. We love you! Along with your father, this book is especially dedicated to you. Always remember we are so very proud of you.

SPECIAL THANKS TO DIANE HAZEN, MY SISTER-IN-LAW

When Diane learned I needed help, that I was desperate for my book to be edited, she set her work aside (she was working as I sent her my chapters) and dedicated days to working on my chapters. My brother, Herbert

Hazen, and Diane live in Wyoming so in the midst of all the preparation needed for harsh winters, the time she dedicated to my book was precious. I love you both and truly appreciate your efforts. Thanks seems such a small price to pay! After hours of work, she sent me corrections that I had not caught.

I thank you Diane with all my heart.

PATRICK SNOW

International Best Selling Author of *Creating Your Own Destiny* and *The Affluent Entrepreneur*

Thank you, Patrick, for your help as my publishing coach in getting my book off the ground—from text written on my computer to a published book available for so many others to enjoy!

You have made a big difference in my life, helping my dreams become a reality in so short a time!

Thank You, Patrick

Visit Patrick at www.CreatingYourOwnDestiny.com

TYLER TICHELAAR

Tyler Tichelaar is my editor and a special man who has been patient in every way with an author writing her first book. I, for one, am excited that such an artist has had the time to edit my book so it could be presented in this wonderful fashion for you to enjoy. I have never met Tyler, except through the email and the telephone, but I feel as though we have become friends through my adventures in writing and our trip to Ireland.

As a way to thank Tyler, I would like to tell you a little about him and his accomplishments.

Tyler holds a Ph.D. in literature from Western Michigan University and Bachelor and Master's Degrees from Northern Michigan University. He is the president of the Upper Peninsula Publishers and Authors Association, a regular guest host on the Authors Access Internet radio show, and the author of numerous novels, history books, and scholarly works.

Tyler is best known for his historical fiction, especially *The Marquette Trilogy*, set in Marquette, Michigan and chronicling the town's history from 1849-1999; it chronicles the lives of pioneers and immigrants seeking to live out the American Dream in the wilderness of the Lake Superior region—there's even an Irish character who came to America as a result of the Irish potato famine! Like me, Tyler has also written a tour book, *My Marquette*, about his hometown and its history.

Visit Tyler at www.MarquetteFiction.com

ACKNOWLEDGMENTS

- Douglas E. Adkins, for your endless time, incredible patience and computer troubleshooting—I love you!

- Kecia Kim (Adkins) Doke, the greatest daughter any mother could ask for—thank you for believing in me. I love you.

- Herb and Diane Hazen, my great family, thank you for your editing/photo editing—I love you.

- John and Lucinda Hazen, your support of my family

Photo of Ha'Penny Bridge
courtesy of Olivier Duc

means so much to me. I wish you could have joined us on this journey, but maybe next time.

- Allan Kane, MD for your incredible patience and editing.

- Marty Wright for your years of support and inspiration and now editing.

- Marie Brennan for your support, time, and incredible patience, not to mention editing support!

- Jane Forrest at Blarney Castle for providing many hours of informational support.

- Anne Behan for the email support you gave me when I was a real nag for information.

- Benita Sinclair of Benita's Bridal Formal & Tuxedo Shop for continuous advice and support with a compassionate hand when needed. Also for taking time out of your busy schedule to help.

- Terry Mestrovich of Headlines for continuous support and interest with my projects over the years.

- Darren Smyth and Geraldine for continued support of what was needed.

- Olivia Waters of Trinity College for the photography identified as theirs and for text provided by their website with permission to reprint/copy.

- Bronagh Kelleher at Fitzwilliam Hotel, for your time, information, and research.

- Olivier Duc for the contribution of photographs found in Chapter 2: Doors, Ha'penny Bridge, Dublin Castle, and the Spire. Thank you for your generous donation to use in my book.

- Peter Zoeller for your photographs of Grafton Street and Trinity College Library.

- Aoife Machen for all the incredible advice for where to find the many places we were trying to learn about in Ireland.

- Paul and Annette for your hospitality in Ireland and gracious time in adding information that I needed about services available for a tour in 2012 should we decide to organize one.

- Paula Cogan for helping me get the facts straight and having patience when working on a special package.

- Jerome and Caoimhe for help in a rush and for being so willing to help with much information. I sure wish I had met you earlier!

- John and Martina for the help you gave me both personally and with information.

- Kelly Beckett for her unending support during months of planning our trip and talking to me about my book with compassionate support. Thank you, Kelly.

- Tyler Tichelaar for your editing assistance. Your kindness and patience was so greatly appreciated.

- Shiloh Schroeder & Jessi Carpenter of Fusion Creative Works (www.fusioncw.com) for my cover design, art work, and web site.

- John and Heather Harbinson, our new friends in Canada! Thank you for the photos you have shared and the memories in Ireland.

- Susan Friedmann, thank you for your assistance with my ISBN and for such a wonderful experience with a publishing company.

- Joanne Gonzales for believing in me and for her plans to host book signings for her literary group. Thank you for being a great friend.

CONTENTS

ABOUT THE AUTHOR

Rosemary Adkins is an author, speaker, and expert traveler within Ireland.

Rosemary "Mamie" Adkins was born and spent most of her childhood in Houston, Texas. Later, she moved with her family to Las Vegas, Nevada, where she graduated from Bishop Gorman High School in 1965. After graduation, her family moved to Redding, California, where Rosemary resided for about six months, until she turned eighteen and fled the state and home. From there, Rosemary became restless and moved around until she found a happy place to be in Eugene, Oregon.

Her childhood had not been the happiest, so she had to deal with overcoming the challenges of abuse, which would affect her life for years to come. She found peace walking the ocean's beaches or swimming in the Gulf. She says of this time in her life, "Whenever I was full of self-doubt, afraid, and lonely, the beach brought me to a place with an inner peace." Happy memories surround the water for Rosemary, which is what later made her journey to Ireland especially exciting.

After leaving home to become independent, Rosemary was still unable to escape abuse, finding it this time in a bad marriage. Haunted by the cycles of life, she ran from her problems, hoping to find someone who would love her; eventually, she found and married her husband, Douglas. Together they raised her daughter and he became her daughter's legal father, making them a happy, connected family, all loving one another. Life was finally good for Rosemary.

In 1985, Rosemary was diagnosed with diabetes, and since then, she has fought the ravages of the disease with many serious complications, but she has managed to come out of the illness to realize her dreams.

In 1997, Rosemary, with her husband and daughter, founded the American Diabetes Association (ADA) chapter in Kitsap County, Bremerton, Washington, and she has organized many educational events, health fairs, and fundraising activities for ADA. An inspiring essay she wrote about her fight with diabetes and how her family and friends have affected her life won her a trip for two to Washington D.C., where she met with several officials, visited the White House, attended a congressional dinner, and was presented with an award for her essay at the Kennedy Center during a special concert by Gladys Knight. Rosemary has also been presented with the Unsung Hero award by her local newspaper, *Kitsap Sun*, with a celebration held in the Admiral Theater for her volunteer work in the area where she lives.

The day arrived that her health had finally become better, and with the devoted help of her husband, Douglas, and the support of their daughter, Kecia Adkins Doke, her dreams once again came alive.

Rosemary had dreamt of writing a book to help others, but she always found it difficult. When the opportunity arose to take a trip to Ireland, Rosemary poured herself into it and studied Ireland for nearly two years. Part of her dream was to pay tribute to Douglas for loving and taking care of her for so long without ever a complaint.

A trip to Ireland felt so right and finally gave her the chance to spend quality time with the man of her dreams in a location that was surrounded by water, the very kind of place that gave her peace growing up! And she had secretly dreamed of repeating her wedding vows at the water's edge and having a new wedding band blessed (Claddagh band) for the years to be shared for the next quarter century!

That trip has resulted in Rosemary, now in her senior years, fulfilling her dream to write a book. *Extraordinary Dreams of An Ireland Traveler* details her and her family's journey to Ireland and offers in-depth information on the history of each location discussed. In addition, Rosemary negotiated savings for her readers when they travel to Ireland.

Rosemary says writing this book has given her insight and motivation to finish another book—a book she started many years ago titled *Mamie* which she hopes to finish in the next two years.

Rosemary resides with her husband, Douglas, and sweet chocolate Labrador, Sandy, in Bremerton, Washington.

She thanks you for reading her book and wishes you a pleasant and exciting adventure, whether it is with her in this book or in Ireland itself!

So come on! Let's travel to Ireland!

Introduction

Extraordinary Dreams of an Ireland Traveler

You've finally made up your mind—that dream vacation can wait no longer! It's time to make plans!

That day came for me on the cusp of my husband Douglas' birthday and impending retirement. I decided to surprise him

with a dream vacation, and the next day I sat at my computer, methodically looking up each of the hundreds of websites I found listed on every search engine!

This trip was to be the granddaddy of them all! It would be a surprise for the man in my life who had kept me alive when sick, my spirits high when I wanted to give up, and my body strong enough to fight an illness that had strangled the life from us throughout most of our marriage. This trip had to be perfect, and I wanted to plan it without help.

First, I looked at tours, then at cheap flights. I researched hotels and read every review ever written, and finally, I got on every mailing list in this country and overseas that offered anything for travel packages lasting from four days to eight weeks. By the time I answered each email, my day was half over.

I decided I could not keep a secret of such magnitude. As I practiced springing my secret on my mother-in-law, my voice was measured and steady, but sounded far calmer than I really felt. She was not sure I could keep something so enormous from her son since I usually shared everything with him. But I kept on planning, and writing to family and friends in hopes they would come along for a giant party to celebrate all the reasons one takes a trip of a lifetime. Our daughter and her husband, Kecia and Jonathan, my mother-in-law, Vonnie, and my brothers, John and Herb, were the only family who supported my plan to surprise Doug. I did get some great advice from my sister-in-law, Diane, so I felt nothing could go wrong. Diane had shared with me how to find medical help should I need it, what not to pack, and tips on how best to tell a loved one a secret that I had withheld from him for so long. With the loving support of my friends Ganelle, Cathy, Nancy, Bonnie, Marty, Rusty, and my doctors it seemed all the hurdles had been crossed in planning the trip without Doug knowing. But...all the advice had been the same in the end—TELL HIM!

It was time to confess. I had not made travel reservations, but had planned out all the details and I was ready to commit. As I prepared dinner that evening, I told Doug that a secret was tearing me apart, and I offered him the choice to know about it or stay in the dark. Doug had wanted to visit Ireland for a long time, and I told him the best surprise of his lifetime would be spoiled if I told him. But he wanted to know.

The rumble of not so distant noises clouded my mind and the turmoil in my stomach was sheer torture. What if, after all the time and energy, all the anticipation, Doug said, "No" to the trip? How would I hold my ground? What could I do if Doug resisted the idea?

Making my case would be easy, or so I thought. I was informed and had been saving money for some time. I'd saved enough to pay for half of the flight and had mapped out payments that would easily pay off the balance within the year. By this time, I had become a fixture in the travel office and knew most people there by name. Thank you, JoAnne, Victoria, Steve and Elizabeth! I knew that AAA Travel Agency allowed you to put your vacations on layaway, and with the proper insurance, you could cancel the trip for any reason without losing any money. I'd done my prep. I was ready for the debate.

But I was sure Doug would find a way to delay all the plans I had been quietly scheming over for months or find a reason we should not plan a huge trip coming right after retirement. But how could you not want to go on such a trip? We had so much to celebrate. His big birthday was near, retirement was close, our anniversary was special this year, and my doctors said I could go! What more did I need to move forward?

The final moment had arrived so I looked Doug square in the eye and blurted out, "We are going to Ireland in June!" Doug just shook his head and asked, "Are you crazy?" I responded by saying that all he had to do was say, "Thank you" and pack his bags. I had done most of the research, and besides, I had already bought him travel gifts for Christmas that could not be returned! Now after I did a little more talking, he soon warmed to the idea of a trip and said, "It might be nice to see Australia!"

AUSTRALIA! But he'd talked about Ireland so many more times. I hadn't done any research on Australia. I knew they had koala bears, kangaroos, and plenty of beaches. Oh my, I did not want to look any further! EEKS, now what? I decided to tell him some of the reasons why I had decided on Ireland rather than Australia in hopes that would finally get us back on track for planning this great trip. I had not wanted to spoil his image of Australia because maybe someday we could travel there as well, but the fact of the matter was that I was afraid to go there. I had read about many problems with traveling there, and basically, I am leery of things I know nothing about. So I explained what I had read and told him that I had run into a few people at the travel agency who had traveled to Australia and what they had told me was a nightmare for them. They and many other guests had been stung by flying poisonous ants while sleeping, causing them to spend time in the hospital. We decided not to push our luck on this trip, and after a bit of discussion, we were on our way together—to IRELAND!

Actually, now that Doug was in on the secret, planning became much more fun. Planning a trip should be done together. Although I had enjoyed putting the trip together, I have to admit some of the research was very dull. I was tired of finding sterile, mind-numbing, lifeless facts that offered no excitement or real advice. Oh how I celebrated when I found fascinating facts that captivated my heart and soul.

During the planning, I found myself reading nonstop—day and night! I read review after review until I could not bear to read any more. And how could I be sure the reviews were sincere and not paid for by some property owner? Doug is good at spotting insincerity, so that alone was reason to have him help me.

In planning your trip, be sure you do not make the same mistakes I did. For one year, the facts of vacationing consumed me. Finding myself either caught on the Internet or in a book every day, every night, and in my partial sleep state was a bit too obsessive. I even dreamed about some of the reviews that were not so great. We wanted to stay in nice properties, some grander than others, but also with families in a bed and breakfast. Bed and breakfasts are a fine way to get to know our friends across the seas. But how can you be sure the hotel is not just a pretty picture, or that a bed and breakfast (B&B) is honest and clean? What about security or privacy in either?

However, one good thing happened along the way. Since I, and then we, had done so much research, we decided it would be a waste not to share our experience. We decided to write this little book just for you, sifting through all the information and recording our trip and the impressions each site left, in hopes of providing information from a different point of view. We wanted to present a book to you that allows you to feel what we felt as our trip unfolded and see through our eyes every enchanting place we visited.

Facts are good, as are opinions, but they can leave you confused, left with too many choices. I know that is what we are offering here since we are discussing the choices we made, but we will honestly tell you when our choice turned out to be sufficient, advantageous, elegant, or simply hideous!

For me, I just kept reminding myself, "Life's a teacher. A mind is the highway. Learning is the reward." With these words echoing in my mind, I decided it was time to begin sharing plans with my friends, family, and you rather than to dream or plan them alone.

After all, if life is a teacher, hopefully, I had been paying attention; if the mind is the highway, only your own thoughts can limit your plans; and, certainly, if learning is the reward, we would not want to stifle our learning process. This made perfect sense as the starting place for our journey!

Our intention in writing this book is to share with you our journey step-by-step, with information and photographs along the way. We will offer you our opinion on what is of value and what could be a waste of your time and money, but remember, these are strictly our opinions.

I think it's important to clarify here that we are not professional writers, travelers, or photographers. We have not been hired or paid by any establishment. We make our judgments on every location, meal, and site we experienced based on the facts of our personal experience and our preferences and emotions. Our lodging was judged by its location, cleanliness, restaurants, pubs, and entertainment. We are also not trained to rate hotels or restaurants. We are simply ordinary people, hopefully like most of you, who enjoy a good meal and clean place to sleep, perhaps with a little elegance thrown in.

In the throes of us planning the most adventurous trip of our lives together, time marched on relentlessly.

Each time a new fact crossed our desk or computer screen, a lump would rise in my throat. Many times I rejoiced over finding the "perfect deal." However, as a word of advice, let me tell you that we missed out on many good deals because we hadn't set a firm departure date. Pick a date and do not waiver. As we have learned, and most books will tell you, the best time to travel is in the off-season. For most destinations, that would be from January to mid-February or spring (March and April), or fall (September through mid-November). But be careful, as many activities are closed at these times of year, depending on your destination. Also the day of the week you travel on makes a difference in flight cost. Traveling on Tuesdays, Wednesdays, Thursdays, or Saturdays are the best choices. Also, in case you have not given thought to international time tables, you will probably lose a day in transit. For example: if you leave Seattle on Tuesday morning flying to Dublin, Ireland, depending on the connection and the directions you travel, you will probably arrive on Wednesday morning. So if you can, allow yourself an extra day for travel.

Finally, be sure to prepare for the weather! We departed for Ireland on June 1st, 2011, and we had no idea of what the weather would be in Ireland since when I checked online, it had been so radically different in the weeks leading up to our scheduled departure.

When we first started laying out our wardrobe, I decided three weeks' vacation called for two pairs each of black, beige, navy, and white pants, two pairs of cropped pants, and two pairs of shorts. Then, of course, I needed both summer and colder weather tops to match and three pairs of shoes, not counting the pair I wore.

With all the luggage needed to contain all those clothes, Doug and I were embarrassed and felt like we were laughingstocks!

PLEASE take my advice. You do not need all these clothes! All you really need is: One pair of dress pants, two pair of casual pants or jeans, and one dress, skirt or pant suit; one sweater, three long sleeve and three short sleeve tops, and enough socks and undergarments for a daily change the first week.

This list is for three weeks, so depending on how long your trip will be, make adjustments accordingly. But anything more is just a waste of space and strength since you have to carry all this luggage around. After all, there are laundromats along the way!

I took two suitcases and did a lot of shopping for friends and family. We wanted to send half of everything home before we left, but we never got to it. I ended up buying another piece of luggage and came home with three suitcases plus carry on! Doug did the same.

Remember, you are on vacation so you don't want to deal with too much luggage. Trust me, you only need one suitcase. And do not fill it up if you plan to shop at all. I am not a casual person for the most part, but I found myself wearing jeans most of the time (they usually do not wrinkle).

At the end of this book, you will find a list of suggestions that will make your life easier as a traveler. There is also information we learned along the way that can be useful for you to know in advance. For example, be sure you get up and move around during the flight, as it is a long trip to Ireland and most physicians will warn of the possibility of blood clots. Although they are a rare occurrence, clotting is a serious risk.

According to several sources, Ireland is today one of the top ten places to vacation. Ireland offers many places to discover, but the thought that some day it could lose its old world charm makes me shudder.

In fact, developers and affluent individuals may even own CASTLES! Yes, I did say castles—there are several for sale. (Laws there are specific in stating that castles must be left intact with no structural changes except for strengthening in order for them to keep their historical values.) While preserving their integrity, they are widely used for "Castle Hotels." You may perhaps not want to castle hop, but you must at least visit one—it will be worth a lifetime of memories!

I must warn you that the Ashford Castle is a five-star hotel and unless you have reservations, they will charge you €5.00 per person to enter the gate, and even then, you will not be allowed to go inside the property but only observe from the outside.

Visiting Ireland, as with any destination can be expensive. However, with diligence and research, you can minimize costs while still experiencing a memorable trip. In addition, we are happy to announce that we have negotiated and can offer you special packages for lodging, site admission, cruises, dinners, and other spectacular savings to various places we visited on our journey and have chronicled in this book.

Please visit our web page at www.ExtraordinaryIreland.com for your direct link to these savings.

So come on and let's take a trip to Ireland together!

View from our seats, flying into the night, sixteen hours from home!

ATLANTIC OCEAN

NORTHERN
IRELAND
BELFAST

IRELAND   IRISH SEA

Ashford Castle
Maam
Cross
GALWAY   DUBLIN

Inis Mor   Lisdoonvarna   Birr
Inis Oirr   Gort   Kinnitty Castle
ARAN   Doolin
ISLANDS   Ennis
Shannon
LIMERICK
Bunratty Castle

Tralee   Kanturk Castle Ruins   WATERFORD
Dingle   Mallow
Fossa
Ring of   Killarney   Blarney Castle
Kerry   CORK

Bantry   Kinsale   CELTIC SEA
Mizen Head   Rosscarbery
Toormore

This map includes locales and main roads we used to drive to towns
and sites that were visited in this book. Many additional roads and
routes are available. Please refer to a detailed map of Ireland to plan
your trip. Although we did not travel directly from Galway to Dublin,
this highway is included for reference .   Map by Diane Hazen

Chapter 1

DUBLIN

We arrived in Dublin on Thursday, June 2, 2011, in the wee early hours of the morning. We had traveled all day and all night. We were tired, but excited—and filled with joy as the landing strip came into focus. You could see that the skies were bright with sunshine and

Flying over Dublin at 6:30 a.m.

the pavement still sparkled with dew as we departed the plane. Our tired eyes scanned the airport, wondering just where we would find our luggage and our ride to the hotel. We prayed our room would be ready for us, even though we were arriving six hours early.

As we approached Dublin Airport, we gazed out on the city, wondering whether the population would be up and moving about. Ireland has a population of just over four million people, one third of whom live in Dublin. WOW! Our adventures would be competing with almost one and a half million residents and thousands of tourists.

Although Dublin is a small city, expect to find a large number of people who are easy to know if you take the time to say "hello." Complete strangers are eager to be helpful and go out of their way to give directions should you get lost, as well as advise you on shopping, and even send you to the best places to eat.

There were many taxis so transportation would not have been a problem, but we were grateful that we had reserved our ride in advance. It is not like in America where a van waits to whisk you off to your hotel! Be prepared to take a taxi. The average fare if your hotel is in the city center will be about €30.00, which, as of August 2011, was $43.00.

Ireland has two major airports—Dublin Airport on the east coast and Shannon Airport near the southwest coast. If you begin in Dublin and depart from Shannon, you will have an excellent opportunity to see a great deal of Ireland, provided you plan carefully.

We heard many tales about going through customs in Shannon, but we found out they were all myths, so do not worry about departing from either airport—in both, you go through security and then have the opportunity to visit the Duty Free area; then you enter customs and go back again through security before reaching your departure gate. But once back in the States, you will go though security AND customs once more. It is a hassle, and mildly inconvenient, but it did make us feel the United States is safe and secure. The whole process takes time, so plan on getting to the airport about three hours, or more, early. You will be happy you did.

In my opinion, Shannon Airport is easiest and best. The rental car location there has more to offer and the staff is nice and cares about your satisfaction with the vehicle you drive away in. You can still plan four days in Dublin and include it as a departure location.

Dublin is a city full of atmosphere—the fresh air and smell from the salt waters surrounds you, and aromas from bakeries and the rich hops roasted in the Guinness brewery immediately embrace your senses.

Dublin is over a thousand years old and history will be all around you. The city is proud of its writers of song, poetry, and magical stories that were created in Dublin but are enjoyed world over. Dublin's youth revel in their history and are involved in preserving their culture, including Irish Dance, which became a favorite of ours. The city is a combination of laid-back lifestyles and a thriving civic center, bustling with commerce and entertaining visitors from all over the world.

Nighttime entertainment in Dublin teems with treasures to discover. Invigorating classical, jazz, and rock music performed by traditional performers is easy to find. We also found that some of the best entertainment came from street performers playing for tips, so watch for people in crowds—chances are they've found something amazing.

Dublin requires at least a four day visit to sample the best attractions and catch up on a bit of rest from your long flight. If you plan your days carefully, you can see most of the major attractions in that time. But you could easily spend more time in this city without exhausting its attractions.

Weather: In June we found the weather to be a mix of sunshine, rain, and wind. I believe that the highest temperature while we were in the Dublin area only reached 60 degrees. We found the weather in Dublin, as in the whole of Ireland, to encompass all four seasons within a day's time so be sure you take along a sweater—or don't and use it as a good excuse to SHOP!

Chapter 2

DUBLIN SIGHTSEEING

FITZWILLIAM HOTEL

The crisp fresh air was a bit chilly with dew still on the ground, but the sun was shining when we arrived at The Fitzwilliam Hotel at St. Stephen's Green.

We were greeted with an alert and compassionate hotel staff that accommodated us very quickly. It was a treat to feel so welcome after a long flight. It felt as though we had never left home!

It was early in the morning, but Dublin was already moving about. The bustle of the new day dawning promised good things ahead for our first day in Ireland.

The hotel was decorated in quiet tranquil decor. The hallways were painted a two tone grey with luscious burgundy carpets

Top: Doug

Center: The Fitzwilliam Hotel Lobby

Bottom: Hotel Room

Rosemary Adkins & Bronagh Kelleher

and an edging of white script lettering using the letter "F" for Fitzwilliam on the border.

The doors themselves were a heavy, dark wood, unlike so many hotels that offer white cold steel doors, giving you a chill as you enter the rooms.

The hallways were most pleasing to the eye and set a relaxing mood even before you entered your room. Our room and the others we observed had the same soft grey colored walls with vivid accents of purple window seating and cushions in matching patterns. Our drapes were fine velvet striped with gold, purple, and burgundy that tied the surroundings together and took my breath away. A handsome bed was framed in tufted purple with a headboard. Some of the rooms even had four-poster beds and private balconies.

Robert Devine and Bronagh Kelleher

You will find the staff outstanding in every department. The head concierge, Robert Devine, and his staff will help you with everything from your luggage to planning your day! Upon checking in, the front desk clerks treat you as though you were a family member they had not seen for some time and are happy to see you! The housekeeping department caters to your every need. Want extra coffee, tea, sugar, or hand lotion—that is not a problem; all you need to do is ask.

Be sure to say hello to the sales director, Bronagh Kelleher, since she is the one who makes sure you have those special extras. She is a person of extreme perfection and integrity, and she is helpful in every way. A hard-working professional woman, she takes the time to ensure all your needs are taken care of and you find everything you need. We later met with her and she helped us put together the perfect offer for your own trip to this fine hotel. Thank you, Bronagh!

This five star hotel certainly earns its rating. It is first class in all departments. Our room was delightful in almost every way—I say almost because I am used to a bit more light and an outlet in the bathroom for my curling iron and those two things were not there. However, in fairness, none of the facilities we stayed in had bathroom outlets. We believe it is a safety feature due to water and plug-ins. Some women pack and use gas curling irons when visiting Ireland.

And don't worry about arriving early in the morning, tired and needing a place to relax—The Fitzwilliam Hotel offers a feature we had never before seen. They have a dayroom you can use to get cleaned up and rest until your room is ready! How easy is that? No extra charge for that luxury either.

We had a complimentary tray of fruit (that came at a perfect time I might add), and most importantly, our room was ready at 7 a.m. Have you ever tried to check in that early anywhere? At almost all of the locations we've visited, you have had to wait to check in later. Much later! In this hotel, they believe arriving guests are tired and need a place to rest and clean up, so they have the dayroom available!

The concierges, Robert Devine and his staff, simply stated, were AMAZING! Our entire stay was just exactly that way down to the smallest detail—even the housekeeping could be called amazing. Whenever we would return, our room had not only been cleaned, but tidied up as well. Items were rearranged on the counters and desk so your room was picture perfect each time you entered. At night, they came back and offered a turn down service and gave us a two piece box of chocolates—a very nice touch. The decor was extremely tasteful and restful in every corridor, room, and lobby.

We had a chance to see the penthouse. Now if you want pampering, this is the place to be—2,000 square feet of luxury!

Top: View of the living area from private kitchen!
Center: Penthouse Master Bedroom
Bottom: Connemara Marble Tub and Shower

So all in all, if you are looking for that perfect vacation, this is it! FIRST CLASS IN EVERY WAY.

We had truly found the place to be in Dublin—where five star hotel did not mean stuffy and pretentious but polite, friendly, buzzing with activity, and exquisite all in one! It was a real treat to have a place to rest for a couple of hours before setting out on our first day in Ireland.

The restaurants in this hotel are rated a Michelin category. The head chef, Kevin Thornton of Thornton's Restaurant and The Citron Restaurant, was featured on the Food Network and is regarded as one of Ireland's top chefs.

A dinner prepared from his kitchen is sure to please the most discriminating critic! You will find an assortment of offers at a value that will both surprise and please you!

THE FITZWILLIAM HOTEL FACTS

- Five Star Hotel
- Ten Years of Age
- 139 Rooms
- 25 percent of business comes from the United States
- Restaurant Rating: MichelinGrade

- Kevin Thornton, Head Chef
  Email Contact: (Bronagh) bkelleher@fitzwilliamhotel.com
- Sister Hotel—The Fitzwilliam Hotel, Belfast

If you want to vacation in style, be sure you do not miss this hotel. There is another property in the middle of the Grafton Street area, but at the Fitzwilliam Hotel you are within walking distance of Grafton Street, and as an added bonus, it's a quiet retreat from the noise of this well-known shopping area.

At present, the Fitzwilliam only receives 25 percent of its business from the United States. However, we feel this is because you do not know about it yet, or you think you can't afford a five-star hotel. But the Fitzwilliam is worth investigating. And don't forget to ask for your special package tied to this book!

The Fitzwilliam is one hotel we hope to visit again, but if you get there ahead of us, please say hello to Bronagh and Robert.

GUINNESS STOREHOUSE

We had reservations to take a tour of the Guinness Storehouse, so we were off and running, not allowing time to steal away our day. I must tell you, as excited as we were to go there, the Guinness Storehouse turned out to be a disappointment. We thought we would be escorted through the storehouse so we could watch different phases of beer making. But it seemed to be just a gathering place for tourists to enjoy a beer, look out picture windows with grand views of Dublin, gaze at

Top: Gravity Bar
Bottom: Guinness Grounds

the fifty acres of grounds where the brewery was producing the Stout, and buy souvenirs.

What you see there, while entertaining, are only areas of water, barley, and grinders where the barley was once ground, and photos of what once was. It was the original site, but the production is not there any longer, or at least not in the building that you can tour.

The current brewery is somewhere on the acreage outside the large picture windows, but nowhere that you could actually see. You walk from floor to floor, seeing more of the same—interesting, but no hands-on brewing. It was disappointing not to see the making of this fine beer. We were told that tours were not allowed for sanitation reasons, yet here at home, we can watch ice cream being made commercially as employees work behind enclosed glass walls. What you do get for your admission fee is a free pint of Guinness!

And, of course, when finished, you are led into the gift shop, where you can buy anything from postcards to beer. We felt our money would have been better spent just lifting a pint in a pub somewhere in Temple Bar. You can at least enjoy the sounds of traditional Irish music there while indulging in a drink and perhaps even a meal. Or just touring the city! There are so many places to visit all over the city that we would have enjoyed more.

GUINNESS BREWERY

The formula for Guinness is not complicated—hops, water, barley, and yeast, but Arthur Guinness took those ingredients and turned them into "Black Gold."

Look for this amazing beer at home, and if you can find it, get used to it before you go to Ireland since it is much stronger there than any beer we enjoy at home!

Doug enjoying his beer with Standing Room Only!

Historical Facts: Records indicate that in 1759, Arthur Guinness at the age of thirty-four signed a 9,000 year lease at a brewery no longer in use at St. James Gate, in Dublin. In 1929, two million pints of Guinness were sold each day. In 1950, five million pints were consumed each day, illustrating

Guinness Storehouse
Honest, I was just holding Doug's beer!

a steady and hurried growth of the company. In 1959, Guinness introduced its Draught beer. In the year 2000, the Guinness Storehouse opened to the public. Statistics tell us that as of 2008, every day over 10 million glasses of Guinness are enjoyed in over 150 countries worldwide.

If you get to Ireland before we return, have one of these famous glasses of "Black Gold" for us too!

HOP ON HOP OFF

We did not want to pick up our rental car until we were ready to depart Dublin at the end of the first four days of our trip

Hop On Hop Off Bus –
Dublin, Ireland, "A Great Value"

through Ireland. Outside our hotel, you could pick up either the rail, taxi, horse, and trap (cart), or cross the street and catch the Hop On Hop Off bus and below you will find a scale for the pricing! This bus is truly a value. The busses stop at more than twenty major attractions around Dublin (which is more than most will ever have the time to see) and when you see something at one of their stops, you simply Hop Off! After you have spent as much time in that area as you want, you go back outside to the bus stop and Hop On one of the busses that comes around every fifteen minutes. Then you either do the loop around again to your hotel stop or ride it around until you are ready to Hop Off again! If you are traveling as a family, this ride in itself, can be entertaining for your children. It truly is a great way to see Dublin.

We enjoyed the seating on these double-decker buses, too, because you can select which way you want to ride—on top in the open air or under cover, or you can sit below, which is fully covered. Kids will love this feature as well. The driver will usually keep you entertained with stories or tell you what you are seeing as you pass it. If you want to reserve anything prior to your arrival in Dublin, this is one you should consider. And may we suggest you get on and take the entire ride around to the different attractions, which takes about one and a half hours, so you can determine which places you want to see the most and make a plan.

Riding the Hop On Hop Off Bus will help you make a plan so you won't miss the things or places most important to you. A rule to traveling is to protect your time and have a plan; otherwise, you may end up wandering around and accomplishing nothing. But above all, enjoy your vacation first!

The Hop On Hop Off Bus Tour seems to be designed (according to one of many drivers) to allow its riders the freedom of leisurely enjoying the history and culture of Dublin. It visits all the main attractions throughout this fair city, taking in Trinity College where the Book of Kells can be seen, the Guinness Storehouse, Jameson Distillery, and Phoenix Park where you can take in the Dublin Zoo.

The amazing tour bus drivers are natives of Ireland and know the area better than most. They will provide you with an informative ride, as well as entertain you with their humor, and they are accredited by Failte Ireland, an Irish tourist corporation. You can purchase tickets for two days and use the Hop On Hop Off all you want, beginning with its first ride at 9 a.m. with twenty-three stops along its route.

If you know where you would like to tour, you may purchase at a discount the tour tickets you will need at the attractions where the buses stop. On the buses, you can also enjoy live commentary in ten languages, and they even provide you with complimentary maps to use so you will not get lost!

Just take a ride all around the area before you decide how to spend your time on the many individual tours available.

Visiting Information:	
The rates are as follows: (as of June 2011)	Adult: €16, $24*
	Student & Senior Citizen: €14, $21*
	Child (5-under14 yrs): €6, $9*
*Prices are subject to change.	

NOTE: Two children under 14 years old travel FREE with one paying adult. Subsequent children traveling must buy a ticket. If you have a private tour group, arrangements can be made for a private booking. You can contact info@dublin-sightseeing.ie for more information.

Places of interest will include the beautiful and very expansive Trinity College where you will find the Book of Kells, which is the main attraction for the College. Dublin's Hop On Hop Off Bus will get you there and many other places that are equally as interesting and moving. In the following chapters, you can read more about these areas, but please be sure you put Trinity College on your list of sites to visit. The Hop On Hop Off Bus can take you there, and you will arrive right at the college's doors.

Other means of transportation are as follows:

- **By Tram:** If you are staying at the Hotel Fitzwilliam as we recommend, then we suggest you consider the Luas (the city tram offering two lines—a red line and a green line), as they are right outside the front door of this hotel. Luas means "speed" and offers an easy way to get around Ireland. A single, one way fare can be around two Euros and with a Smart Card pass for weekly, round trips you can save even more. Due to several trams moving on the same track, your wait time is short.

Timetable/Contact Information:	
Website:	www.luas.ie
Phone:	1800 300 604
Email:	luascustomercare@veolia-transport.ie

Following are different ways you can travel around the area:

- **By Sea:** The Port of Dublin offers six ferry companies for cross channel services to the UK and is an easy five minutes from the City Center.
- **By Train:** You can connect with many locations with the train system. They also offer day and overnight tours so you can stay based in Dublin.
- **By Rental Car:** There are a number of rental agencies, but we recommend you use the ones based in Ireland rather than companies such as Hertz or Avis as they offer a nicer selection of automobiles and at better rates. Sixt and Argus are among the best to use.
- **Ireland Bus Service:** Bus Eireann is Ireland's national bus system and provides many routes into Dublin city and around the country, including Northern Ireland.

Public Transport Operators in Dublin:

- **Dublin Taxis:** There are thousands of taxi drivers within Dublin City who are more than happy to transport you to practically anywhere in the city.
- **The Dart:** This is the city's Rapid Transit System Network. It travels along the coast of Dublin and surrounding areas with services into the heart of the city.
- **Dublin Bus Service:** The public transport system in Dublin is Dublin Bus with over 140 routes and more than 1,000 buses providing service for most locations in and around Dublin. These double-decker buses can be identified by their blue and yellow colors.
- **Bus Fares in Dublin:** To avoid crime, the buses only accept payment in the correct amount. No change is given for overpayment, but they will issue you a change ticket to be redeemed at the Dublin Bus Headquarters located on O'Connell Street.

If you will be commuting more than once on Dublin Bus, there are a number of different pre-paid tickets you can purchase, such as:

- A Rambler Ticket: a single and multi-day ticket option
- Adult (Bus & Rail) Short Hop

- Family (Bus & Rail) Short Hop
- Adult One Day Bus/Luas Ticket
- Child One Day Bus/Luas Ticket

These buses are wheelchair accessible, making them handicap friendly. You can check online or on their schedule for the handicapped bus schedule.

> **Tip:** Because each bus stop is serviced by more than one bus route, when you see the bus approaching, you must signal in time for them to stop or they will not!

Getting Off: Each bus has handrails where you will find buttons to press that will alert the driver of a stop request. Be sure to give the driver plenty of notice before the stop.

Dublin Bus Services: A number of different services are provided by Dublin Bus, apart from the normal public routes. These include:

Dublin Bus to Airport Services: More than 700 bus services are servicing the airport daily, with routes to the city center and far away destinations like Cork, Belfast, and other major locations with some buses running seven (7) days a week. Fares vary with each route and locations. Time tables are posted online for your convenience.

DUBLIN SIGHTSEEING!

The next few days were spent exploring the streets of the city centre, Grafton Street, St. Stephen's Green, Temple Bar, O'Connell Street, and looking at all the historical buildings we could find time to visit. Below are photos of some of the areas we will visit in the next few pages!

GRAFTON STREET

Visiting Grafton Street was some experience! Staying at The Fitzwilliam, we just had to walk out of our hotel, take

Temple Bar Area

Top: Christ Church
Bottom: O'Connell Street

a left down the sidewalk, stroll about 100 yards, and we were in the busiest shopping area in Ireland.

Strolling down Grafton Street, you can sightsee, eat, grocery shop, buy anything you want, and be entertained all at the same time! Now, that is a treat to say the least.

I have read reviews that state Grafton Street is like a busy mall or any large city's shopping strip, but that is simply not true. I would like to know where else you can shop for hand-knit woolen goods, grocery shop, dine, buy fine jewelry, be entertained for free, or stop in for a drink all in the same place. This is one area in Dublin where you can be entertained every other block like in no other part of the city.

©Peter Zoeller

No, Grafton Street was not like anywhere we had ever been before, and we would love to go back there just to look around, people watch, and be entertained! You can spend the day there for free, or literally, shop until you drop. Now, in all fairness, although we stayed at The Fitzwilliam Hotel and simply loved every detail about it, you can also stay in the middle of Grafton Street at The Westbury Hotel.

The Westbury Hotel's website describes it as: "a Dublin landmark, synonymous with luxurious elegance. Step out of its front door and within minutes you can be wrapping yourself in designer brands on Dublin's Grafton Street, or immersing yourself in the black stuff with a trip to St James's Gate and the Guinness Storehouse."

There is no doubt that Grafton Street is Dublin's finest shopping mecca. Designer clothes, cosmetics, and perfumes, prominent jewelers, and shoes are everywhere! Not just shoes, but great quality shoes—I wish I had waited to buy a new pair there so they would have been different from what is here at home.

There is anything and everything there—even pharmacies with the most knowledgeable pharmacists I have ever met. I injured my foot while walking and, of course, on a weekend, so I went to a pharmacy and asked for help. When I told the pharmacist I was a diabetic, he said he would look at my foot and tell me whether I needed emergency care. This was a major help for us. All was well; his advice was easy to follow and his help made me feel secure.

Giftware is abundant too along Grafton Street. From ties, tweeds, sweaters, throws, crystal, diamonds, body shops, bath shops, treatment spas for your feet, camera shops, pet stores, grocery stores, telephone stores—so many things it would take pages to list them all. Need a bank? It is there, too.

A mall called St. Stephen's Green Shopping Centre is at the top of Grafton Street where you can find just about everything I've already listed all over again. This Georgian Shopping Centre offers many fine aspects found nowhere else, so along with the Grafton Street area, much is available and an entire day can be spent there.

Still more—check out the next centre at the bottom of the street. Avoca is a mini-department store with a seven level mini-department store featuring fashions for men, women, and children, along with household items and even a cafe. We did not get that far since I was tired, but a clerk along the way told us all about it. We had shopped in probably every store, had a few drinks along the way, listened to entertainment, and watched performers the entire day from morning until dusk, so for us we now had to call it quits.

Grafton Street is a one mile stretch with thousands of pedestrians crowded onto the street at all hours, and if you do your share of shopping, it will feel like you have walked fifteen miles by the end of the day. However, vehicle traffic is no concern since the street is closed to autos. Serious shoppers— this is for you! Don't forget to stop in at a coffee shop for a break—many people suggested Bewley's to us, but it was too crowded for our tastes.

ST. STEPHEN'S GREEN

St. Stephen's Green is a rectangular park with approximately twenty-two acres in Dublin's City Center; it is said to be the largest of the parks in Dublin's main Georgian squares. It was designed and created in 1664, is maintained by the Office of Public Works, and is open all year.

As we walked through the park, we observed many people sitting on the lawn picnicking on this lovely day with its grand peaceful surroundings. If you don't wait until dark and plan ahead, why not pick up a lunch and take it the few minutes' walk to the St. Stephen's Green Park for a delightful picnic by the ponds.

A Gift from Germany to Ireland—
April 28, 2005—
St. Stephen's Green

Ardilaun Lodge is a lovely home currently occupied by the groundskeeper, according to a sign posted on the front lawn. It is the most sought after house in Dublin because it is located in the southwest corner of St. Stephen's Green.

Behind the lodge to the right is the Unitarian Church, which is said to be a popular place for second weddings.

We thoroughly enjoyed our casual walk through St. Stephen's Green. Although there

are traffic lanes surrounding the
park, it is not a busy thoroughfare for automobiles. Many
pedestrians walk the park and
surrounding shopping area of
Grafton Street or the St. Stephen shopping center.

The bordering streets are all
named St. Stephen's Green with

St. Stephen's Green at the Pond

North, South, East, or West added on as appropriate. The offices of many
public bodies and the city terminus of one of Dublin's Luas tram lines is
also found here and stops in front of The Fitzwilliam Hotel. The nearby
shopping areas would include the Fitzwilliam Square and Merrion Square.

May we suggest you either have your hotel pack a lunch, or you can visit a
market located on Grafton Street for just about anything you could need
and return here for a picnic by one of several ponds where the ducks are
highly visible.

TEMPLE BAR

Temple Bar area is to Dublin
what The French Quarter is
to New Orleans! Each has its
own special attributes that give
its city character! The French
Quarter has its Bourbon Street
Blues and Temple Bar has its
traditional sounds of Ireland.
The two should be sister cities.

Photograph taken at Gogarty's Pub

You will find cobbled streets and old buildings in the Temple Bar area. In
1991, Temple Bar was entrusted to Temple Bar Properties Limited, which
was expected to develop thriving homes with cultural and business ties to
attract visitors in large numbers. Here we want to share the highlights of
Temple Bar!

We saw many areas that strangers on the street would stop to tell us to get out of as quickly as possible, assuming we were lost, because the area we were walking in was rough. I must say, I at no time felt afraid or thought we were in trouble. This area of Dublin was colorful, loud, and a place to spot many unique individuals.

We were hungry and wanted a drink, so we wandered into Gogarty's where everything was great. Doug had his first Irish Stew (lamb), sharing a bit with me, of course. It was fabulous! Although we had grown to dislike lamb at home, we knew it was widespread in Ireland, and we had vowed to try a little bit of whatever was served to us. You should all do the same! It was really good, and we believe we had not liked lamb before because we did not really know the proper way to cook it.

I had the fish. Nothing unusual, but although it was fried, it was not greasy at all. The chips were also not greasy; I was so surprised that I asked what their secret was! The staff said it was because they used everything fresh and cooked the potatoes fresh and never from a frozen state. When I later tried this at home, it was not greasy, but fresh!

So, our tip from Temple Bar is: Do not be afraid to try any new dish at least once!

Gogarty's was hopping with business and people were coming and going. They had a live band playing the ole Irish tunes. The only thing missing was the dancers! This is one place you do not want to miss. I can promise you one thing about Gogarty's—you will NOT be unhappy about any part of your visit there. Meals are divine and priced to fit any budget and the entertainment is free!

You can look them up: www.gogartys.ie or telephone them at 01-671 1822. The country code for all of Ireland is 353 but each area has its own area code, so be sure to double check before you call. The cost for us when we called from Washington state for forty minutes to Blarney was only $4 so do not be afraid to call Ireland. Just be sure to check your rates first!

Here is the address on how to contact Gogarty's for reservations, should you want to contact them.

Contact Information:	
Website:	http://gogartys.ie/pub
Pub Opening	10:30 a.m.—2:30 a.m. Mon-Sat
Hours	12:00 a.m.—1:30 a.m. Sun
	Carvery Lunch 12 noon—4 p.m.

Should you want to stay in this fun spirited area where the budget is at a lower cost, Gogarty's offers both a B&B hostel and apartments that will sleep six people. They are located in the heart of Dublin Cultural Quarters, known as Temple Bar, and have a reputation for offering an award-winning restaurant with traditional music seven days a week. It may be a bit noisy for you since they are always busy. They are open from 2:30 p.m. until 2:30 a.m.

PUB LIFE

Next tip: Eat your meals in a pub since the food is great and inexpensive.

Check out the pub crawl tour, should you want to be with a group or do it yourself. The advantage of the tour is that you are guaranteed a seat!

Live music can be found almost everywhere.

You will find more than one thousand pubs in Dublin, all with their own flare for entertainment, whether it be music, storytelling, or, most certainly, conversation. Some of these pubs date back to as early as

Pub Life

1666! You can expect the best advice for planning a day for visiting pubs or anywhere else from the locals.

Pub life in Ireland cannot be compared to any other place on earth that we have ever heard about. It is a way of life, not just as an escape from day-to-day problems, but for socialization and mostly conversation. An Irishman's

generosity of spirit is priceless, and he is usually eager to assist you with any inquiries about most things. The Irish people's dry sense of humor is difficult to understand at first, but once you overcome it, you will find yourself smack in the middle of genuine teasing. What a hoot!

When you look up the definition for a pub in the dictionary you will read that it is a meeting place for people to share their stories, tales of yesterdays, and future dreams. We must not forget that gossip is certainly bred here as well! Pubs can also be a grand stand for solitude, debates, lovers, and even violence.

Friendships that last for lifetimes and are even passed onto the next generation are quite often acquired in the local pubs. The myth has it that one never drinks alone in an Irish pub, but that very same myth has it that a friendship is proven by how well you can take a joke!

The best of pubs are said to be those with stone floors and peat burning fires, where laughter and song can be heard for miles around! We certainly found that to be true in most of the pubs we visited on Temple Bar.

One night we joined up for laughter, drinks, and entertainment with what is known as a "Pub Crawl" we booked through the tour company Viator (many other tour companies and options are available as well). This is definitely an activity you won't want to miss since it is not easy on your own to find the pubs that offer traditional Irish traditional with a dance performance for entertainment.

On our pub crawl, contagious laughter, tales, (and big ones at that!), and conversations made our entire evening enjoyable. We found spirited, filled rooms in every corner of this well known district day and night. Although, for the record, after the sun goes down, you will definitely find a bit more freedom in the atmosphere!

During the pub crawl, we joined up with a group from Sweden. They said they had been many places in the world, and we talked with them about seeing all the amazing old sites. One woman responded that she had seen enough old places and was so happy to be in this pub where people were not so old. The joke was that we were all in our senior years! So it goes to show you that a friendship, or at least a conversation, can be started up anywhere, with anyone, and at any time! Enjoy yourself—you are on vacation.

In the daytime, you will find Temple Bar buzzing with foot traffic because it is a major shopping center, but by night, it is a mecca for entertainment from traditional to jazz and everything in between. The pub life is laid back but buzzing all day and evening, and eating in pubs is a great way to experience Ireland's most traditional way of life at any time.

Portes De Dublin by Olivier Duc

O'CONNELL STREET

Rising to become one of the British Empire's most prominent and prosperous cities, Dublin flourished in the early eighteenth century. Elegant Georgian homes were built beyond the walls of the medieval town. The first development was named Merrion Square, where all the exterior doors were painted the same color. We heard on the Hop On Hop Off Bus that painting all the doors a different color began when a man named Moore decided to paint his door green to keep another gentleman named Gogarty from knocking on his door at night when he had had a bit too much to drink and mistook Moore's house for his own. Gogarty, angered, painted his door red! That sounds like a fun version of the why the doors are different colors, but the truth later came out on the bus and it goes like this:

> Every unit was built exactly the same with strict rules by the developer, but the owners of these Georgian homes wanted to have their own touch so they added special door knockers and painted their doors whatever colors suited them, with red being a favorite color.

> In the 1950s, the Irish government tried to destroy the reminders of the colonial past so many Georgian homes were destroyed. The Irish Tourist Board, historians, preservationists, and architects fought to stop this movement and succeeded. With tourists flocking to take photos, these doors became "the famous doors of Dublin."

> Now, we also heard the story that when Prince Albert, Queen Victoria's husband, died, everyone was ordered to paint their doors black in mourning, but the Georgian home owners rebelled and painted them different colors.

Which story do you like the best?

Back to the history of O'Connell Street!

In addition to the doors, monuments to Irish leaders can be found on O'Connell Street.

Daniel O'Connell was a leader of the independence movement in the mid-nineteenth century. He was elected to parliament in 1828 when he also fought in London for the Irish Catholic emancipation (to be free from control). The emancipation repealed the restrictions many Catholics lived under because they were not Protestant like their English rulers.

O'Connell was known as "The Liberator" and O'Connell Street was named after him in 1922. O'Connell apparently had a great love for both Rome (having lived there) and Ireland since when he died, he had his heart buried in Rome and his body in Ireland. That implies to me that he loved Rome but felt loyal to Ireland.

The main bus lines stop on O'Connell Street where you'll find major shopping attractions, the central post office, and cinema. Some sources on the Internet suggest you will not find the nicest people on O'Connell Street. But we have to say that we met only the very nicest people almost everywhere we visited. However, you may not want to visit this area after dark because at night it reputably becomes the wildest street in Ireland where you will most likely encounter people with drugs. Now we did not check that out!

However, in the daylight you certainly do not want to miss this main street in Dublin. It is a commercial street with much history that surrounds and runs through it. You will find the statues of Irish heroes from Charles Stewart Parnell, for whom Parnell Square was named, Daniel O'Connell (O'Connell's statue took nineteen years to complete!) and Jim Larkin, a famous trade union leader. The O'Connell monument still stands with bullet holes from the Easter Rising in 1916 when Ireland was striving to gain its independence from Great Britain.

We wanted to learn about some of these historical facts before visiting Ireland to help us decide what we wanted to see. If you are intrigued by history, here are a few facts you may find interesting:

O'Connell Street is the largest street in Dublin and said to be one of the largest streets in the whole of Europe. The street is mostly commercial, but it is worth the time to see its landmarks. The General Post Office dates back to 1818, and became part of history when in 1916, Irish leaders used it as headquarters during the Easter Rising and Patrick Pearse read the "Proclamation of the Irish Republic" from the front steps. During the uprising, the building was

Photo courtesy of Olivier Duc

mostly destroyed except for the façade, allowing it to be rebuilt to preserve a piece of history.

In 2003, a monument was built called the Spire of Dublin. It stands almost 394 feet tall, making it the world's tallest sculpture.

O'Connell Street (formerly known as "Sackville Street" and still known as such by some residents) is almost impossible to miss as it is a main thoroughfare and one of Europe's widest streets. Most visitors will want to be sure they don't miss it.

Photo Courtesy of Olivier Duc
olivier.duc1@gmail.com

DUBLIN CASTLE

A Royal Treat to Tour

Dublin Castle was established in 1204 A.D. and has been at the forefront of Ireland's history ever since. The castle has been a prominent host to meetings for state of the art conferences and the place to dine prestigious guests for centuries. Guided tours are available and the State Apartments are among the most sought after and prestigious in the country.

Visiting Information:	
Opening Hours for Tours:	Monday to Saturday 10:00 a.m. to 4:45 p.m. Sunday 12:00 noon to 4:45 p.m.

Just prior to our arrival, Dublin Castle hosted a dinner for Queen Elizabeth II and the Duke of Edinburgh. This was the beginning of a four day visit to the country, the first time the Queen had visited the Republic, and the first royal visit of such a nature since King George V had visited in 1911.

President Mary McIseese hosted a state dinner in the Dublin Castle on the evening of May 18, 2011 with special guests Taioseach Enda Kenny, British Foreign Secretary William Hague, British Prime Minister David Cameron, and the Irish Minister for Foreign Affairs, Eamon Gilmore. It seems that

May and June were good months to be in Ireland. Even the President of the United States visited Ireland during that time for reasons unclear to me so I won't speculate on his visit!

As for Queen Elizabeth, she said it right during her visit: "Together we have much to celebrate: the ties between our people, the shared values, and the economic, business and cultural links that make us so much more than just neighbors, that make us firm friends and equal partners."[1]

Her words rang true for us because in our hearts that is how we felt prior to our trip and even more so afterwards. "Together we have much to celebrate"—so true.

As tourists, we had much to celebrate because, first of all, a trip to Ireland is a trip of a lifetime, and second, we made friends with our neighbors living thousands of miles from home and exchanged a great experience with almost every person we met. We felt we had created special ties through those friendships, both made for pleasure and business. We have shared values with those special people who made our time in Ireland so wonderful, and between the Irish we met and ourselves, we became equal partners in our new friendships.

"A Grand Long Look is Exactly What You Need"
Photo Gallery courtesy of O.P.W.
Dublin Castle

So Queen Elizabeth, thank you for saying it so right!

Have you ever wondered what is served at such a dinner for royalty? What do you serve a Queen and a Duke?

Just to satisfy your curiosity, I have copied the menu for both the dinner and entertainment from Dublin Castle's website. It was a grand dinner, but

1 Taken from Dublin Castle's website: http://www.dublincastle.ie/HistoryEducation/ TheVisitofHerMajestyQueenElizabethII/FullTextofTheQueensSpeech/#d.en.16153

you will find these sorts of meals in four and five star hotels throughout Ireland, so we can all feel a bit like royalty.

Ireland, I love the way you make so many people feel special. Wouldn't it be nice to be so pampered in such fine surroundings?

MENU

Cured salmon with Burren smoked salmon cream and

lemon balm jelly, horseradish and wild watercress,

Kilkenny organic cold pressed rapeseed oil

Rib of Slaney Valley Beef, ox cheek and tongue

with smoked champ potato and fried spring cabbage,

new season broad beans and carrots with pickled and wild garlic leaf

Carrageen set West Cork cream with Meath strawberries,

fresh yoghurt mousse and soda bread sugar biscuits,

Irish apple balsamic vinegar meringue

Irish Cheese Plate

Tea and Coffee

ENTERTAINMENT

Playing on the arrival of Queen Elizabeth II (Battle-axe Landing)

Liam O'Flynn—Uilleann Pipes

Denise Kelly—Harpist

After dinner entertainment:

A performance of traditional Irish music and dance.

This short performance features many of the most distinctive forms and instruments associated with Irish traditional music. The opening and closing sections include dancers performing several traditional dances with reels, hornpipes and slipjigs. A song entitled "Eleanor Plunkett" composed by one of Ireland's most famous composers, Turlough O'Carolan, featuring voice and harp, forms the central section. The melody is performed in the sean-nós style (translated as old style) and is a unique element of the Irish tradition.

For information regarding the specialized tours at Dublin Castle visit:	http://www.dublincastle.ie/History-Education/EducationalResources/SpecialisedTours/#d.en.15054

If you do not have a computer, contact the Visitors Center in Dublin for more information regarding this castle and any other properties you may wish to visit in Ireland.

Dublin Castle has surely seen its share of prominent leaders who have touched the hearts of many. If you allow yourselves the time to experience the actual surroundings of where you are and let it take you back in time to the yesterdays that were there, you will come away a different person.

Before we leave Dublin Castle, here are a few fun facts about its history:

Although Dublin Castle was established in 1204, "there is archaeological evidence of a wooden and stone castle there in the 1170s." Now wouldn't it be interesting to reside on the remains of another life before yours thirty years earlier? Or would it? This castle, like so many others, comes with a history of hard times, war, and bloodshed, so are there ghosts who lurk in the halls of this grand old beauty? Just our own thoughts—Don't miss this delightful tour so you can decide for yourself whether you can feel the presence of days gone by!

Dublin Castle went through changes over its many years. For nearly two hundred years, it was neglected and became (in the words of the Dublin Castle website) "ruinous, foul, filthy, and greatly decayed." A thirteen-year building program began and by 1570, the moat had been repaired and several new parts had been built. Sadly, however, a disastrous fire in 1684 destroyed much of the medieval castle. Records have been discovered indicating that Dublin Castle was in transition in 1728, and heading for a new Georgian era look, including the now popular State Apartments, which were again renovated in 1746. Shortly thereafter, Dublin's growth made it the second city of the British Empire.

One would speculate that with such a history, the castle and its occupants would be sympathetic to the hardships of its surroundings. Sadly, during the Great Famine of 1845-1849, castle residents continued to celebrate with lavish balls and dinners, as two million people suffered outside the gates.

In 1916, tragedy and bloodshed struck again with the Easter Rising that led to the end of British rule.

After Jim Connolly, one of the rebel leaders of the Easter Rising, surrendered, he was held in the State Apartments until his execution; this room still remains and today is known as the James Connolly Room. Following his execution, there was an outpouring of public support and once again war was at hand—the "War of Independence."

In December 1921, a treaty was signed ending English colonial rule and twenty-six counties became the Free Irish State (Republic).

Dublin Castle has survived the Civil War, transition to Irish nationhood, and its fall into despair. The castle has also been modified and restored into Irish society where it now is host to European Union Presidents, Heads of State, and leaders of business, industry, and government. It is also one of Ireland's main attractions, welcoming visitors from all corners of the globe.

Thank you, Ireland, for such an interesting history lesson, Dublin Castle, and a grand tour.

We also want to express our sincere thanks to Olivier Duc for his photographic abilities and his generosity in letting us use the outside photograph of Dublin Castle and several other photographs in this section of the book.

If you should want any of his well-known prints, his email address is olivier.duc1@gmail.com

"A MAJESTIC LOOK INDEED"

Saint Patrick's Hall

"This is the grandest room of the State Apartments, and contains one of the most important decorative interiors in Ireland. Formerly the ballroom of the Lord Lieutenant's administration, today the room is used for presidential inaugurations. It is one of the oldest rooms in the castle, dating from the 1740s, though its decoration largely dates from c. 1790, including the most significant painted ceiling in Ireland executed by Vincenzo Valdre (c. 1742–1814). Composed of three panels, the ceiling depicts the coronation of King George III, Saint Patrick introducing Christianity to Ireland, and King Henry II receiving the submission of the Irish Chieftains."[2]

St. Patrick's Hall is the most important ceremonial room in Ireland. It is used for important State functions (such as the State banquet for Queen Elizabeth of England in May, 2011) and the Inaugurations of Irish Presidents. The banners along the walls are those of the now defunct Knights of St. Patrick and include the Royal standard—a symbolic relic from Ireland's colonial past.

Bedford Tower was completed in 1761, and became the centerpiece of the "new look" Upper Castle Yard. It is acknowledged that the north side of the courtyard presents one of the most beautiful architectural compositions in Dublin.

"The Bedford Tower of 1761, comprises the centrepiece of the Castle's principal Georgian courtyard, flanked by the gates of Fortitude and Justice. It was from this building the Irish Crown Jewels were stolen in 1907."[3]

---

2 Material taken from the Wikipedia en.wikipedia.org/wiki/Dublin_Castle
3 Material taken from the Wikipedia en.wikipedia.org/wiki/Dublin_Castle

From this entrance to Dublin Castle, we at first thought we had stumbled into a relic with no personality! What a terrible misjudgment we had made! This is only one way into the courtyard. It is only when you look up and over the roof line that you can see the tower, or Castle Tower, which makes your opinion turn around so you just have to go in and take this spectacular tour!

JAMESON DISTILLERY

Jameson's is located in the heart of Dublin. The distillery takes you back in time. It takes very little imagination to see the happenings of years past. The Jameson's tour begins with a film presentation about the distillery's history and process; it is followed by a walking tour that recreates historic brewing processes. You will learn about Triple Distillation as you tour the romantic past of Irish whiskey making. The tour ends in the Jameson Discovery Bar, where you will enjoy a complimentary glass (shot) of whiskey and even have a chance to take the premium tasting tour, which allows you to taste several different varieties of Jameson whiskey. Then you can become what they call a "Qualified Irish Whiskey Taster," which we did and received a certificate to bring home.

Visiting Jameson's was a nice experience because it gave us a chance to learn more about whiskey on a one-to-one basis. You could do that on

your own, of course, but then you would lose the ambience of this occasion! We also had lunch in the Discovery Bar and enjoyed its delightful soup and sandwich combination. If you so choose, several other entrees are available. Our largest complaint about this experience is that we could not get into the shindig where entertainment, a three course dinner, drink, and tour were in one package. We booked early (four months in advance, but still they were sold-out), so if you take this tour, plan way ahead of schedule!

Angels Share

This photograph is a visual aid to show how the whiskey darkens as it matures. The explanation for the whiskey's disappearance as it ages is that the angels take their share! Look at this photograph beginning on the bottom left side so you can see how, as the whiskey matures, its color changes to the last stage on the top right.

Visit www.jamesonwhiskey.com and click on "Launch the TV Ad" for an online tour with a real sense of humor! Be sure to see the "Spirit We Share" as well.

Of course, as with every other place that has a tour, Jameson's also has a gift shop. It is a very nice place to shop, but it is easy to get carried away. Shop carefully—there are other locations where you can find the same merchandise for the most part, except for the fine assortment of gifts with the Jameson name on them and the whiskey bottles you can have personalized.

This was an interesting tour, but again, there was no hands-on anything there so you could see the actual making of whiskey. While we enjoyed the Jameson's tour, we felt it was another disappointment that, as with the Guinness tour, we didn't have an opportunity to see hands-on brewing; instead we saw only pictures on the wall, short film clips, barley, and some old equipment. We were told again that it was due to sanitation safety, but I have to wonder why it could not be viewed through glass windows as it was when we later visited the Waterford Crystal tour. It felt as though we were in a tourist attraction with the focus on the huge gift shop selection. For the record, when at the Jameson Distillery, the whiskey they sell "only at the distillery" is actually available as well at the airport—just not personalized. And Jameson whiskey is a sure find in every pub!

We did learn a lot about whiskey, which was a plus for this tour. If you visit Jameson's Distillery, be sure to ask about The Shindig, which is a more popular tour because it offers a full evening of a three course or more dinner, a private tour of the facilities, premier whiskey tasting, and live entertainment that includes the Traditional Dance performers.

Now for a bit of Jameson's history:

SINE METU, meaning "Without Fear" was the motto awarded the Jameson family for bravery in fighting pirates on the high seas back in the 1500s. John Jameson took this motto and moved to Dublin in the 1770s to make his place and legacy in this world and his whiskey. I believe John must have been a rebel of his own type. At that time, Dublin was already known for producing the finest whiskey in the world, and John Jameson was brave enough to make his own mark. As an outsider to Dublin, it seems that he believed he could make a difference—and he did!

Jameson Whiskey is distilled three times for exceptional smoothness so you receive the smooth taste of whiskey without that bitter aftertaste. It is said that this is the difference between Jameson's whiskey and those made in the USA, which are distilled only once, and Scottish whiskies, which are distilled twice.

To clarify for those readers unfamiliar with what distillation involves, the Merriam Webster Dictionary defines distillation as: "the process of purifying a liquid by successive evaporation and condensation." Hopefully, that is clearer for you than me—I only know that Jameson's makes a very smooth whiskey.

This process, or tradition, was begun at Jameson's in 1780 by John Jameson himself. He worked hard to bring a balance so it gave a natural barley flavor. John did not want to make just another whiskey, but the number one Irish whiskey in the world.

Now, I probably shouldn't mention it here, but Bushmills is another fine Irish whiskey. We did not get to Northern Ireland to visit its distillery, but we hope to on our next visit. We were offered some Bushmills whiskey in Ireland and it is delightful. We now have it in our cabinet at home!

DUBLINIA:
MEDIEVAL HISTORY

Dublinia is a museum about Dublin's history, and it offers three different exhibits about time periods most people in Dublin never think about today. The exhibits teach you what the lives of Dublin's citizens were like throughout history and the trials they endured just to live and survive. The exhibitions will appeal to all generations in your family.

Top: Viking and Sword
Bottom: Moss As Toilet Paper In Dublinia

A convenient passageway from Dublinia to Christ Church makes this visit one where it's easy to tour two locations. We recommend you purchase a combined ticket so you can explore both.

Viking Dublin Exhibition

This exhibition will take you back to Viking times in Dublin where you will learn about life onboard a warship and life as it was for a Viking. You will learn about the Vikings' voyages, weapons, and what is was like to live in those times and learn of the legacies they left behind.

Medieval Dublin Exhibition

Traveling back in time can be an experience you will truly enjoy if you put yourself into the surroundings, sights, and more. You will learn about the ways of crime and harsh punishments, warfare, the ravages of disease and death, and what it was like to be a rich family versus a poor one.

History Hunters Exhibition

History Hunters (archeologists) are the very back bones of discovery. Through their efforts, you will learn how even the dirt and bugs can solve the mysteries of yesterday. Observe the artifacts of a medieval skeleton and look at the maps of the earliest times in Dublin, giving you insight into what was. Learn how wonderful it can be to discover answers through researching the smallest details in the earth.

St Michael's Tower

This viewing tower of the seventeenth century was said to have once belonged to the church of St. Michael the Archangel, which once stood where Dublinia now sits. If weather allows, you can access this tower by climbing ninety-six steps to view the City of Dublin. Be sure to wear the proper footwear since the climb is steep, but when you get there, you will see the River Liffey and a beautiful and informative view of Dublin.

On your Dublinia tour you will discover about 400 years of the history of Dublin, beginning with Strong Bow and his knights in 1170, to the burning of the monasteries in 1540, under the command of Henry VIII.

Scale models of the street, merchants' homes, and the medieval town are on view. The models explain how the Vikings played a huge part in Dublin's history, beginning with when they first arrived and how they settled in Ireland.

The areas of Dublin, Waterford, Wexford, Cork, and Limerick were major trading areas for the early settlers. Again, when you use your imagination and allow yourself to travel back in time, the history will surround you, and perhaps you will see how it must have been to live in those times.

If you need help imagining medieval times, Dublinia has costumes and armor you can don so you can see what it must have been like to carry around that much weight every day; "throwing rotten eggs and vegetables at a criminal locked up in the pillories" (of course these are soft plastic balls); and three dimensional displays with hands-on activities. The staff tell you not to be shy and let yourselves and children enjoy this activity and have a lot of fun in the process. This is a great outing for your children and a chance for them to learn with you.

Dublinia is open year-round and offers a wide range of activities so you can explore this Viking World in any season; costumed guided tours are also available for schools as part of Dublinia's Living History program.

General Information from Dublinia's Website	
Address:	St. Michael's Hill, Christ Church, Dublin 8
Telephone:	01-679 4611
Email:	marketing@dublinia.ie
Website:	www.dublinia.ie
Location:	Situated in Dublin City Centre, adjoining Christ Church Cathedral
Season:	All Year. Open daily except Dec 23-26 & Mar 17
Open Times:	Apr-Sept: Daily: 10:00 a.m—5:00 p.m.
	Oct-Mar: Daily: 10.00 a.m.—4:30 p.m.
Tours:	Change frequently, check website
Average Visit Length:	45 minutes to 1 hour
Entrance Fees:	Adult: €7.50
	Child: €5
	Student/Senior: €6.50
	Family: €23 (2A+2C)
	Group Rate: €4.95 (includes Christ Church)
How To Get To Dublinia:	Dublinia is located on St Michael's Hill, opposite Christchurch Cathedral. The 123 bus from O'Connell Street or Dame Street stops on High Street in view of the Dublinia building. Just walk back 100 meters on High Street and turn left, walking down St. Michael's Hill toward the River Liffey. The entrance to Dublinia is to your left.

I hope you will enjoy this tour because it is a fine educational part of history, and you will have a great time sharing this part of your trip with your children should you be traveling with them.

Except for the tower, I found it to be a handicap friendly tour.

CHRIST CHURCH CATHEDRAL

Christ Church is formally known as "The Cathedral of the Holy Trinity."

Christ Church is located in what was the former heart of medieval Dublin. As a result of demolition of streets, it is now isolated behind civil offices along the quays and is one of the three cathedrals that can be seen quite clearly from the River Liffey. It was declared the seat of both the Church of Ireland and the Roman Catholic archbishops of Dublin. Believe me; it is very difficult to find a way to photograph these two buildings due to traffic flow and the way they are laid out across the landscape.

The cathedral was founded sometime after 1028. The first bishop was Donat. For a time he was answerable to the Archbishop of Canterbury

in England rather than to the Irish Church hierarchy. The cathedral was originally staffed by secular clergy and was once only one of two churches for the entire city. In 1163, the second bishop of Dublin introduced the Benedictines. In 1172, the church itself was built to impress St. Laurence O'Toole and was to reflect the symbol of re-emerging Irish rule, according to some.

References tell me that the last Catholic Mass said in this ca-

Christ Church Dublin

thedral was held in 1689 (a brief period of Catholic rebirth) in honor of King James II of England.

Christ Church is Dublin's only real cathedral. The close by St. Patrick's Cathedral lacks a bishop, which is required before a church can be designated as a cathedral, and the nearby St. Mary's is classified as a "pro-cathedral" (a parish church used as a cathedral) for political reasons. This leaves Christ Church in a unique position, along with the fact that it is not known by its correct name, "Cathedral Church of the Holy Trinity." From 1871 to 1878, George Edmund Street, with the sponsorship of a distiller, extensively renovated the cathedral. The tower was rebuilt, the flying buttresses were added as a decorative attraction, and the north porch was removed and replaced by the baptistery. A covered footbridge connected the Synod Hall. The cost was over $26,000,000, and the cathedral went through additional renovations between 1980 and 1982. Due to the building's Victorian and medieval renovations, which were preserved from complete ruin, it is difficult to determine which parts of the interior were completed when.

Christ Church holds prominent events, but remains the center of worship for the United Dioceses.

Many places in Christ Church are off limits to cameras, including the impressive solid gold plates located in the basement, where we also watched a live play.

Be sure you visit the area beneath the Cathedral for a look at the medieval crypt and other fascinating sites. This is a huge area where you will find some interesting exhibits and certainly an area you do not expect to see. The exhibits will surprise you because they seem out of place in what looks as though it may have been a dungeon.

As Dublin's only cathedral, one of Dublin's oldest buildings, and a building with elements of medieval architecture, Christ Church is a unique and amazing place to visit. You do not want to miss this tour. Be sure to look up times for the church's services since they will affect your tour and you do not want to miss any part of this historical find.

Visiting Information:	
Christ Church Hours of Operation (as of September 2011):	9:30 a.m. to 5:00 p.m. Early opening for June and July 10:00 a.m. to 5:00 p.m. April to September 10:00 a.m. to 4:30 p.m. October to March
Cost:	check your bank for current dollar exchange rates
Admission prices:	Adult: €7.50 Student: €6.50 Senior: €6.50 Family (2 adults & 2 children): €23.00 Child: €5.00

MOLLY MALONE

Most Americans and other visitors to Ireland will have heard of Molly Malone, or at least know the lyrics to the popular song about her. However, just in case you don't know the song, you are bound to see her statue in Dublin when you visit, so here are the lyrics:

In Dublin's fair city, where the girls are so pretty
I first set my eyes on sweet Molly Malone
As she wheeled her wheelbarrow through streets broad and narrow
Crying cockles and mussels alive a-live O!

A-live a-live O! A-live a-live O!
Crying cockles and mussels alive a-live O!

She was a fishmonger and sure it was no wonder
For so were her father and mother before
And they both wheeled their barrows through streets broad and narrow
Crying cockles and mussels alive a-live O!

A-live a-live O! A-live a-live O!
Crying cockles and mussels alive a-live O!

She died of a fever and no one could save her
And that was the end of sweet Molly Malone
Now her ghost wheels her barrow through streets broad and narrow
Crying cockles and mussels alive a-live O!

A-live a-live O! A-live a-live O!
Crying cockles and mussels alive a-live O!
A-live a-live O! A-live a-live O!
Crying cockles and mussels alive a-live O!

This song, known as "Molly Malone," "Cockles and Mussels," or "In Dublin's Fair City" has become so popular that it's known as the unofficial anthem of Dublin! The statue of Molly Malone was erected in 1987, and dedicated in 1988 by the Lord Mayor of Dublin, Alderman Ben Briscoe, during Dublin's millennium celebration, June 13th became celebrated as Molly Malone Day—an official holiday.

So is Molly Malone's story fact or fiction? Myth or not, it is clear that her reputation, or legend, is adored by most people in the area. As I think back to looking at the statue and how she appeared, I can almost hear her sing out those famous words, "Cockles and mussels, alive, alive O!"

Molly Malone is a human interest story I could not leave alone, so now for a new take on Molly Malone! This version of her story is ours, inspired by so many other tales and the love for such a heartfelt story about a woman taken so early in life. The tales makes you wonder whether she had a happy ending, so if this version of the story is not already written, then it should be!

Who was Molly Malone? Was she genuine or a legend? The statue that sits on the corner of Grafton Street and the stories you read certainly make you want to believe that this reportedly beautiful young girl was as real as you and me. She was reported to be sweet, bringing grace and sunshine to the lives she touched and gladness to the hearts of all who knew her. A small frail young girl with long light-red hair, she was a fishmonger like her parents, but she had a smile to light her way! Yet some said she led two lives—one by day and one by night. Was that jealousy or fact? You decide for yourself.

Who's to know which story is true about Molly Malone—was she chaste or a lady of the evening? But most will agree that she is one of the most famous people in Dublin's history. Was she Fact or Fiction?

If you have not seen this statue, pay close attention to the details. She is well-endowed and the cleavage shown leaves little to the imagination. This does not seem to embarrass anyone because everyone loved this hard-working young woman!

It is said that one man truly loved Molly Malone and deeply mourned her passing. He was said to have loved her more than most and even pined away his life for her. Pierre (perhaps fictional as Molly was thought to be by some) was at the time a street bum singing for tips tossed into his old opera hat. He was also said to have been the abandoned son of a Frenchman and a poor Irish waitress. It is said he used to stand in the area where he knew she would come to sell her fish, and when she came by, he would tip his hat and sing a love song just for her. This went on for some time until one day she did not show up with her sunshine happiness. He remembered she had looked ill for days before, so he became worried and began to look for his true love to confess his feelings. Pierre had not realized she was so ill and it threw him into the depths of despair to learn he could not help her. Still trying to get to her, he ran into the streets for what seemed an eternity, but arrived too late—she passed before he could confess his love to Molly Malone. Fact or Fiction?

Pierre nearly lost his mind from grief seeing her face and was haunted by her voice, hearing it singing out "Cockles and Mussels, A-live a-live O!" one minute and being silent the next. He decided to set sail for England and found passage on a tourist vessel, but he ended up in Belgium instead. There he took a job working at a restaurant washing dishes and doing other odd jobs. He saved his money and chose not to talk to or befriend anyone while still grieving for his love, Molly Malone!

It is also said that he became a man of many talents building himself a large Tudor home and a restaurant chain of fine dining, and even venturing to the Riviera. He chose never to date any other woman. (It's said he never dated Molly Malone either—just loved her from afar.) He never sang again after Molly died, until one night while serving a dinner, he believed he heard her voice cry out as she ordered a house special (a fish platter), "Cockle and Mussels alive, alive O!" and while his eyes caught her hair shining in the light, with tears of joy running down his cheeks to see his precious Molly Malone, he found the voice he had lost for so many years and sang the romantic song from years gone by! Now, is this Fact or Fiction?

The sadness over her death was also reported to have an effect on opera houses all over Europe that paid their respect by performing operas for one month nonstop as a charity for the poor in her honor. Again, Fact or Fiction?

Many tales exist about Molly Malone (some very twisted indeed), including that she was a sweet, hardworking young girl selling her fish by day and her body by night, yet dying young, but again, was this Fact or Fiction?

Being a romantic at heart, I would like to believe Molly was a sweet young girl, who because\she was poor, could not get medical help when she was ill and passed away with a fever caused from working too hard when she should have been resting. I believe Pierre did love her with an innocent heart, and I hope today the two of them are together celebrating life as it should have been for them back then.

Now, that is my version of the tale, but the truth will probably never be known.

Recently, an article in the Dublin *Independent*[4] stated that the song was believed to be a lampoon of the Irish and written in Scotland without Molly being historical at all.

---

4 http://www.independent.ie/national-news/molly-malone-was-written-to-lampoon-irish-claims-expert-2920563.html Saturday, October 29, 2011

Professor Daithi O hogain, from University College Dublin, believes that the popular folk song, which was written in Edinburgh in 1883, by James Yorkston, was likely to have been penned to lampoon the Irish.

He said: "In the concert halls during the Victorian era, various races were ridiculed to a certain extent. 'Molly Malone' may have been composed in Scotland to mock Irish people and their songs.

Whatever the truth, as long as this sexy statue exists, Molly Malone still entertains the tourists, men and women men alike. She is probably photographed more than any other woman in history. Take your photos of her while in Dublin or pose with her for your memories and your own tales!

Wouldn't we all like to have known Molly Malone so we could know the truth? It's up to you to decide whether she was fact or fiction.

TRINITY COLLEGE

When we visited Trinity College, I at first thought we were just going to look at another college campus and the old document written about in every tour book called the Book of Kells, but I had no idea what we were about to experience. The campus was a sprawling property with architecture as magnificent as can be found anywhere in Ireland. This college was founded in 1592.

For a reason I can't explain, the opportunity to view the Book of Kells brought tears of amazement to my eyes. In my opinion, these documents should not only be written about in every tour book, but every hotel room in Ireland should have information about them. The Book of Kells is an illuminated manuscript of the Gospels, and seeing these beautiful Testaments created a feeling that swelled in my throat and eyes while making my heart pound. A positive flow of energy filled the room, and you could see it in everyone's eyes. We were looking at true history!

The other exhibits included tapestries, literature, and photographs of what used to be.

As we continued through the tour (self-guided, which we enjoyed best), we came across the library where documents and medical theses were on display. There you saw skeletons, old and crude medical instruments, and thousands of medical books that lined floor to ceiling in bookshelves that went on forever!

"Overwhelmed" is the only word to describe the feeling.
Photograph by Peter Zoeller

After you complete this incredible journey through the past, pay a visit to the gift shop where you will find unusual gifts and postcards and just that special item to take home that you may never run across again in Ireland. We found postcards, silk scarves, traditional items and many other articles of interest that made their way home with us! You truly do not want to miss this attraction. It is not just another college campus!

The following information is taken directly from the website for Trinity College so you have the benefit of learning why this is such an impressive tour to take.[5]

Photography courtesy of Trinity College

"Trinity was founded just before the Tudor monarchy had completed the task of extending its authority over the whole of Ireland. The idea of an Irish university had been in the air for some time, and in 1592 a small group of Dublin citizens obtained a charter from Queen

---

5 Photograph copyright of the Board of Trinity College Dublin. Certain parts of the facts in this section were taken directly from the Trinity College web page at www.tcd.ie with permission.

Elizabeth incorporating Trinity College juxta Dublin. The Corporation of Dublin granted to the new foundation the lands and dilapidated buildings of the monastery of All Hallows, lying about a quarter of a mile south-east of the city walls. Two years later a few Fellows and students began to work in the new College, which then consisted of one small square. During the next fifty years the community increased. Endowments, including considerable landed estates, were secured, new fellowships were founded, the books which formed the beginning of the great library were acquired, a curriculum was devised and statutes were framed.

The second half-century of the College's history was a time of turmoil, marked in Ireland by an interregnum and two civil wars. In 1641 the Provost fled, and two years later the College had to pawn its plate; some Fellows were expelled by the Commonwealth authorities, others were excluded at the Restoration, and in 1689 all the Fellows and students were expelled when the College was turned into a barrack for the soldiers of James II. But the seventeenth century was also an age of ardent learning; and Trinity men such as Usher, a kindly polymath, Marsh, the orientalist, Dodwell, the historian, Stearne, who founded the Irish College of Physicians, and Molyneux, the correspondent of Locke, were typical of the adventurous and wide-ranging scholarship of their day.

The eighteenth century was for the most part a peaceful era in Ireland, and Trinity shared its calm, though at the beginning of the period a few Jacobites and at its end a very small group of political radicals seriously perturbed the College authorities. During this century Trinity was the university of the Protestant ascendancy. Parliament, meeting on the other side of College Green, viewed it benevolently and made generous grants for building. The first building of the new age was the Library, begun in 1712; then followed the Printing House and the Dining Hall; and during the second half of the century Parliament Square slowly emerged. The great building drive was completed in the early nineteenth century by Botany Bay, the square which derives its name in part from the herb garden it once contained.

These buildings expressed the ordered vigour of the College's life. Unlike the English universities Trinity took its duties seriously. The Fellows were hard-worked, both as teachers and administrators. The curriculum was kept up-to-date, there were quarterly examinations at which prizes were granted to successful candidates, and the fellowship examination was a Homeric contest. Most of the outstanding Irishmen of the eighteenth century, including Swift, Berkeley, Burke, Goldsmith, Grattan and Tone, were Trinity graduates, and the influence of their university is discernible in their writings and speeches.

Three of the eighteenth century provosts were outstanding. Richard Baldwin (1717-58) was a strong disciplinarian who strove to prevent the boisterous high spirits that characterised contemporary Anglo-Irish society from playing havoc with academic peace. His successor, Francis Andrews (1758-74), was a member of parliament and a widely travelled and popular man of the world, whose taste and social ambitions are reflected in the Provost's House, erected in 1759. He provided in his will for the foundation of a chair of astronomy and an observatory. He was succeeded by John Hely-Hutchinson (1774-94), a barrister and an enlightened if self-interested politician. Eager to widen the curriculum, he was responsible for the foundation of chairs of modern languages, and he pushed forward the eighteenth century building programme. His sometimes not over-scrupulous approach to College problems involved him in wrangles with many of the Fellows, and his provostship is the Dublin equivalent of Bentley's stormy and litigious mastership of Trinity, Cambridge.

The history of Trinity College can be divided into four epochs—a century or so during which the foundations were laid, a period of colorful expansion extending over the eighteenth century, a consolidation and advancement in the nineteenth century, and a century of strenuous adaptation to a rapidly changing world.

So far as Trinity was concerned, the nineteenth century began only when Bartholomew Lloyd became Provost in 1831. A determined if conciliatory reformer, his provostship was marked by a number of important changes, of which the most significant was the introduction of the modern system of honor studies in 1833. Until then there had been only one course for the degree of B.A., the ordinary or general course in arts embracing classics, mathematics, a little science and some philosophy. It became possible for an undergraduate to specialize when in 1834 examinations for degrees with honors, or moderatorships, were established in mathematics, in ethics and logics, and in classics. In 1851 a moderatorship in experimental science was added; this at first included physics, chemistry and mineralogy, and was later expanded to comprise geology, zoology and botany. In 1871 it was divided into two, moderatorships being given in natural science and in experimental science. This arrangement was maintained till 1955, when the two groups were again combined in a moderatorship in natural sciences. In 1856 a moderatorship was founded in history and English literature, which continued till 1873, when separate moderatorships were instituted in history and political science and in modern literature. In 1961 a moderatorship in English literature and language was introduced. The introduction of these moderatorship examinations was accompanied by the development of honor courses and of a system of 'honor privileges' which eventually enabled honor students to substitute honor for ordinary lectures, and honor for all ordinary examinations except the Final Freshman examination, or 'Little-go'. The abolition in 1959 of 'Little-go' for honor students completed the separation of the honor from the ordinary curriculum; since then the ordinary course in arts has undergone several revisions and was finally discontinued in 1978. Two-subject moderatorship courses, instituted in that year, now offer alternatives to the single honor more specialized courses.

The nineteenth century was also marked by important developments in the professional schools. Divinity had been taught from the foundation of the College, and in the nineteenth century its teaching was systematized. The Law School was reorganized after the middle of the century. Medical teaching had been given in the College since 1711, but it was only after the establishment of the school on a sound basis by legislation in 1800 and under the inspiration of Macartney, the brilliant and quarrelsome anatomist, that it was in a position to play its full part, with such teachers as Graves and Stokes, in the great age of Dublin medicine. The Engineering School was established in 1842 and was one of the first of its kind in the British Isles. The School of Commerce was established in 1925, and the School of

Social Studies in 1934. In 1962 the School of Commerce and the School of Social Studies amalgamated to form the School of Business and Social Studies. The School of Pharmacy was established in 1977. In 1969 the several schools and departments were grouped into Faculties as follows: Arts (Humanities and Letters); Business, Economic and Social Studies; Engineering and Systems Sciences; Health Sciences (since October 1977 all undergraduate teaching in dental science in the Dublin area has been located in Trinity College); Science. In 1977 the Faculty of Veterinary Medicine was transferred to University College, Dublin.

This expansion of the College's activities had an outward sign in the buildings erected after 1800. Just after the middle of the century, the New Square was completed by the erection of the Museum Building; and new buildings at the east end of the College Park expressed the increasing importance of the natural sciences and of medicine in the life of the College.

Between 1830 and 1900 twenty new chairs were founded, and Trinity scholarship displayed to the full the versatility, the industry and the self-confidence of the Victorian age. The Trinity tradition, which, even in an age of increasing specialization favored a wide range of interests, had a stimulating effect on members of the College. Towards the end of the nineteenth century the School of Classics could boast not only classical scholars like Palmer and Purser, but also men such as Tyrrell and Mahaffy, whose interests ranged from ancient Egypt to Georgian Ireland, and Bury, whose Byzantine studies straddled the classical and modern eras. In mathematics and science there were Rowan Hamilton, Humphrey Lloyd, Salmon, Fitzgerald and Joly. In English there was Dowden, a sensitive critic and an irascible politician, and in economics Ingram, the most outstanding of the Irish positivists.

It would be a mistake to picture these men and their colleagues as working in an undisturbed academic calm. Momentous changes were taking place in Ireland, and these were reflected in the controversies that raged round the government's Irish university policy. Between 1873 and 1908 schemes were proposed by the government of the day which would have made the College a member of a federated university, in which several other Irish academic bodies would have been included. These schemes were strenuously and effectively resisted by Trinity as threats to its independence. On the other hand the College progressively abandoned the exclusive religious character that, in common with Oxford and Cambridge, it had hitherto borne. As early as 1793 Roman Catholics had been permitted to enter and to take degrees in Trinity. In 1854 non-foundation scholarships, open to candidates of all denominations, were instituted. In 1873 all religious tests, except those connected with the Divinity School, were abolished.

In the government of the College the last century has witnessed far-reaching changes. The creation in 1874 of the University Council, a representative body, gave control over the shaping of courses and appointments to the teaching departments. From 1900, as can be seen from the evidence given before the royal commission of 1906, the composition of the Board was being strongly criticised by important sections of College opinion, and in 1911 the constitution was modified by the addition of two representatives of the Junior Fellows and two representatives of the non-fellow Professors to the Board. The representation of the Junior Fellows was increased to four members in 1958. At the same time the Statutes were altered to require that half of the professors should be Fellows.

Strange to say, one innovation of far-reaching significance aroused relatively little controversy. In 1904 women were admitted to the University and by 1914 they already amounted to 16 per cent of the students on the College books. In 1908 a women's hall of residence, Trinity Hall, was founded. In 1934 the first woman professor was appointed and women continue to play an increasing part in many spheres of College life. In 1968 women were elected to Fellowship. From 1972 men and women students have resided in the College and at Trinity Hall.

The Great War of 1914-18 marks in more than one way the end of an epoch for Trinity College. When conditions again became settled Ireland had undergone a constitutional revolution and the College found itself in a divided Ireland outside the United Kingdom. Moreover, at a time when the newer universities in the British Isles were growing in strength and prestige, Trinity College found itself lacking in the resources required to maintain its position in the new age. In 1920 a royal commission recommended that the College needed both a large capital grant and an annual subsidy. But the change of regime occurred before its recommendations could be implemented, and it was not until 1947 that the College secured an annual grant from the State. The grant now represents approximately 53 per cent of total recurrent income (excluding research grants and contracts). Between 1900 and 1999 ninety-four new chairs have been created.

In recent years student numbers have risen well above what had come to be considered the norm. In 1998-9 they stood at 13,700 as compared with 1,500 in 1939. The increase in numbers has brought greater diversity, with students coming from as many as 70 countries and often spread over all six continents. Demand for places from Irish applicants has progressively reduced the vacancies available to non-Irish students. In 1998-9 the undergraduate intake was about 90 per cent Irish: the proportion of non-Irish students to be admitted in the future will not, it is hoped, fall below 10 per cent of the total annual admissions. There is no restriction on the number of postgraduate or one-year students subject to availability of places in certain areas. This change in the composition of the student body has been accompanied by a similar change in the composition of the academic staff. Until the nineteen-thirties, the great majority of the holders of academic posts in Trinity College were doubly indigenous, being Irishmen and Dublin University graduates. But since 1945 many of those appointed to the staff have come from other universities. Probably this is one of the factors which accounts for the accelerated pace of change, which has been a striking characteristic of the period since the end of the war—change reflected in an increase of the representative element on the Board, in a radical recasting of the arts curriculum, in the erection of new buildings and the adaptation of old buildings to new needs, in the improvement of College rooms and the provision of new amenities for undergraduates, in the extension to women of those privileges previously reserved to men, and in the institution of joint student-staff advisory committees covering most aspects of College life."

Trinity College has a website where you can view photos in their gallery. Sorry for no photos of the Book of Kells, but none were allowed. Be sure when you visit this property that you buy these photos from the gift store in a postcard or other means so you have a record of memorable visits!

Here is your free link to more photographs of fabulous Trinity College:

http://isservices.tcd.ie/avms/photocentre/gallery1.php

Chapter 3

WICKLOW MOUNTAINS
The Ones We Missed

This story was a sad one for us at the time, but looking back, although still upsetting, it is at least no longer a tragedy! It is a story that is now a bit humorous, but I must say, we were not laughing at the time.

It took a great deal of time to pick up our car as it seems everyone else was departing Dublin this beautiful day. (Or at least we had hopes that the day would be beautiful!)

On our scheduled departure date from Dublin, we had taken a taxi from our hotel to where we were to pick up our rental car and prepared ourselves to travel to the Wicklow Mountains. We were looking forward to enjoying their beauty which we had read and heard about before arriving in Ireland.

On our way to pick up the car, the taxi driver asked us where we were headed. When we told him, with delight in his voice, he told us of the huge sweet strawberries that were being sold this time of year all over that area. Being a lover of strawberries, I could hardly wait to get there. He told us that the car rental people would tell us one way to depart from their area, but to be sure to go in another direction to avoid traffic.

The car rental was packed with people everywhere, with lines so long there was standing room only. We were so embarrassed about all the luggage we were lugging around because now all we could do was scoot it inch-by-inch across the floor as the lines moved while people watched us with amazement in their eyes. One person even commented that they had almost as much as we did—thank goodness we were there for three weeks and they were there for only ten days—somehow that made me feel a lot better.

Well, after spending two hours picking up our car and fixing the problems there, we were off! We had set the GPS for the Wicklow Mountains and expected to be there in about an hour. By following the GPS, however, it was two hours before we finally passed a road sign that told us we were going the wrong way! We were going in the direction for Cork on a highway that bypassed the direction we had planned on going. We were nowhere close to the Wicklow Mountains—we had missed them entirely. We soon realized the GPS was messed up; it kept taking us in the wrong direction and showed us driving along the side of the road when we weren't!

Not only had we missed these special mountains, but we had missed our strawberries, too. We searched the rest of the trip for these kind of strawberries, but they could not be found—only small ones were on the market and they were not sweet at that!

Lesson learned: TAKE your own GPS! Just buy the program you need for it and use your own.

Because we planned to see the Wicklow Mountains, we at least want to tell you a bit of what we learned about them. Because we did not get there, this information is compiled from Internet sources rather than personal experience. We feel visiting the Wicklow Mountains is a worthwhile trip, so be sure not to miss them like we did!

The Wicklow Mountains National Park was established by the government in 1991, and it is managed by the National Parks and Wildlife Service.

They run in a north-south direction from south County Dublin across County Wicklow and into County Wexford. Lugnaquilla is the highest peak in the range at 925 m (3035 ft), and Mullaghcleevaun at 847 m (2,780 ft) is the second highest.

The southern limits of the Wicklow Mountains are set by Croghan Mountain, the highest point on the Wicklow-Wexford border and the scene (in the nineteenth century) of Ireland's only Gold Rush.

These reportedly beautiful mountains are located in the Glendalough Valley spread across Wicklow, Dublin, Carlow, and Wexford Counties. The monastic settlement of Glendalough was believed to have been founded by St. Kevin and has now become a popular tourist attraction as well as the Powerscourt Waterfall, the highest waterfall in Ireland. The mountains occupy the entire centre of County Wicklow. These exquisite mountains are made up of granite and quartzite.

The whole area is greatly frequented, especially on weekends, by Dubliners because it offers multiple forms of recreation from fishing to rafting and hill walking.

The weather is reported to offer the outdoors person a mild damp summer and cool wet winters. These mountains, together with the rivers that run through them, provide the drinking water for Dublin. The mountains also provide a natural haven for rare birds while the valley has a strong growth of vegetation.

I recommend you do some research and find this location on a map so you don't miss the Wicklow Mountains like we did. If you have a computer, go online and search for images of Wicklow Mountains, you'll find some stunning images.

I'm sorry we don't have our own photos of this region, but you know our reason!

Please enjoy your trip to these mountains and enjoy a strawberry for the two of us!

Chapter 4

WATERFORD

WATERFORD TOWN

The port city of Waterford, in the county of Waterford, was founded in 914 AD by the Vikings, making it the oldest city in the country. Waterford means either "ram fjord" or "windy fjord." It is the largest city on the southeast side of the

"Amazing Treasures" Commissioned Piece

country and the fifth largest city in the Republic of Ireland.

To experience the true ambiance of Ireland, be sure to discover for yourself the city of Waterford, its many bountiful beaches and its remote areas like the Comeragh Mountains.

Waterford is a city for all ages. We especially enjoyed the tour of the House of Waterford Crystal because the glass was actually being blown right before our eyes!

Also of primary interest is the Port of Waterford, one of the most active in Ireland and containing Waterford's historic shipyards. Many of the ships carrying Waterford Crystal around the world were built by Waterford's own shipwrights.

Waterford has been building ships for more than one thousand years. The most famous ship built was the *SS Neptune* in 1846. This iron steamship was 172 feet long and weighed 326 tons. When it was built, it was the largest ship of its kind in Ireland. The *Neptune* sailed into the Russian port of St. Petersburg to carry a gift of Waterford Crystal Glass to Tsar Nicholas I.

Spreading out from the port, the city's architecture represents a restoration of its heritage, making it a mix of old and new, with its people following their ancestors' trades and keeping Waterford's historic past alive.

Waterford's climate is typical of this island nation, with mild and changeable weather patterns, moderate temperatures, and plenty of rain. Waterford is known as the Sunny Southeast with June, July, and August being the hottest months. Temperatures range from around 63-68 degrees Fahrenheit with a low of 46-53 degrees, so pack a sweater for evenings.

Waterford gets more sunshine than most cities in Ireland, but it gets rainfall all year round, with the wettest months in the Fall/Winter (October, November, December, and January).

WATERFORD CRYSTAL

Waterford is world renowned for its crystal and touring the Waterford Crystal Company's factory is one tour you simply do not want to miss!

Waterford Crystal Company claims that its crystal's durability is unmatched, and I can attest to its beauty. There is little doubt that you will want to save up for this tour as you will, of course, want to bring home several pieces—don't worry, they will ship it home for you!

The company is struggling against difficult times because of the economic problems worldwide. But the company has remained strong for over two hundred years and it continues to produce the world's finest crystal. You must give credit to the Irish themselves for this success. I can attest that throughout our trip we met people who had been through hard times yet seemed to be strong and remained positive in spirit and perseverance! The story of Waterford Crystal should be an inspiration to us all.

This clock was designed by William Maddock, a watch and clockmaker in Waterford and is on display at the beginning of the tour at Waterford Crystal. It is handcrafted in Waterford Crystal and is upwards of 200 years old—an amazing piece to see! We took this photo during our tour in June 2011.

Waterford Crystal got its start in 1783 when it was founded by George and William Penrose. They launched the crystal business with £10,000, which converts to about $16,000. In the eighteenth century that was an enormous sum of money, but they were world class businessmen and took the gamble. The Penroses began with less than 100 employees, but head craftsman, John Hill and his crew soon produced the finest crystal in all of Ireland and England. John Hill was a compounder and designed the original Waterford Crystal. The crystal became the initial building block of trade for Waterford, making it the busiest port in Ireland, exporting crystal as far away as New York and the West Indies.

"The William Maddock Clock" The first piece seen on the tour

When John Hill became friends with a clerk named John Gatchell, he taught Gatchell his techniques for making fine crystal before leaving the company. When Hill left, Gatchell took over as head compounder. In 1796, William Penrose passed away and the company was sold. John Gatchell remained as one of the new partners and became the head of the company fourteen years later. Things were not easy for Gatchell because Ireland passed a new tax law imposing heavy excise duties and the entire glass industry struggled, but his dedication and relentless efforts paid off, and Waterford Crystal not only survived but thrived throughout his tenure. Twelve years later, Gatchell's son, Jonathan, took over the head of the company—Waterford glassworks—and kept his father's work alive for another sixteen years.

The Irish excise tax had destroyed many glass companies, taking down eight of the eleven. Although the government reduced the tax, it was too late for many companies. In 1851, the Waterford Crystal Company was sold again after being held by the Penroses and Gatchells for sixty-eight years.

This is the first area of the factory tour, which is Mould making. The fire is behind the men here where the glass starts out. The craft of mould making is much the same as it was centuries ago. We were able to watch as they shaped the glass into crystal using wood moulds and hand tools! The wood moulds and hand tools are made from beach and pear wood, which are better able to tolerate high heat. However, the heat causes the moulds to wear out quickly, so they are replaced every seven to ten days.

Blowing Department

Nothing compares to watching ordinary glass blown into a masterpiece. What starts out as a piece of glass goes to the furnace, and then this man takes it to the wood mould and turns and blows it into shape. This is an awe-inspiring moment, the first of many on this tour! The furnace is 1,300 Celsius, which is 2,372 degrees Fahrenheit! You will be amazed at the blowers' skill as you watch the molten crystal take shape as it has for two hundred years—right before your very own eyes! This is why Waterford Crystal is the best tour in Ireland—you actually get to SEE it happen.

Quality Inspection

Pieces are inspected at each stage of production. Only pieces that pass the company's rigid standards make it to the next stage. Each piece is subject to six separate inspections, and if it fails at any stage, it is destroyed and returned to the furnace for re-melting. Waterford Crystal does not sell any second-rate products.

Hand Marking

This next department is critical—as all the departments are in their own right, but here you will watch as the crystal is hand marked with a temporary grid to aid the Master Cutter in cutting the pattern onto the crystal piece. Cutters learned and memorized each cut pattern during many years of training. If memory serves me, that apprenticeship lasts for at least eight to ten years! The temporary mark will be removed during the cleaning process. If you look closely, you can see the hand marking on the vase (black) that the cutter uses.

Cutting Department

Two types of cutting techniques are used at Waterford—the Wedge Cutting and Flat Cutting. An industrial diamond wheel gives a high quality and cut to the crystal, but the craftsman has to gauge the pressure he uses to cut the designs, and if an error is made, the piece will be destroyed. Craftsmen are responsible for each piece's clear and sparkling cut—the distinct hallmark of Waterford Crystal.

Sculpting & Engraving

Sculpting

Crystal Sculpturing is done with a wheel by the Master Sculptor working three-dimensionally on solid blocks of crystal. This process can take days

or even months. This is why Waterford Crystal is expensive—but not excessively so when you consider the labor of love and the skill needed to achieve the crystal we all love and desire to own!

Engraving

This is where the specialty pieces are prepared. A copper wheel, called an "Intaglio," which means reverse, is used for engraving. The engraver cuts deep into the crystal for a more prominent appearance, which is used for the International sporting trophies and limited edition inspirational pieces.

In 1947, the company was revived with a new factory built about twelve miles from the original location upon which Penrose had built more than a century and a half earlier. Today, the main factory is located on a forty-acre site and there are two other plants in County Waterford as well. The three sites employ thousands.

At Waterford Crystal, they insist on perfection, which is why, in my opinion, each and every piece is priceless. I simply could not come home without the Seahorse which is their mascot.

Although we were there for the tour, most of this information was taken from the Waterford Crystal website at www.WaterfordVisitorCentre.com. Enjoy!

Finished Pieces

Photos taken at the factory when we were taking the tour.

Chapter 5

CORK

RIVER LEE HOTEL

Our visit to Cork began at the River Lee Hotel where we found ourselves wrapped in luxury at affordable prices. If you are looking for a four-star hotel with every amenity possible, this is the place for you. Parking is available and the English Market is within walking distance for those who do not mind a fairly long, leisurely stroll.

The absolutely grand River Lee Hotel is a property hard to beat in Ireland. Fortunately for us, we had managed to select locations throughout Ireland that we loved and want to revisit!

As you approach the River Lee Hotel, you may think you are about to enter a cold, uninviting place with an equally unfriendly staff, but allow yourself to be surprised. For one thing, this was the first place we visited where we didn't have to worry about parking or the safety of our vehicle. The lobby was mammoth and yet gave us the feeling of being quietly embraced by elegance. To the right, the seating beckoned you to take a rest. Further in, off to the right, was a long hallway leading to a bar, restaurant, and offices. Coming in the front door to check in was a long entrance that was also inviting and quietly decorated with a soft color scheme. The front desk staff patiently waited for you to approach and then swiftly got your

room keys and escorted you to your room, should you want or need help. However, we chose to walk ourselves so we could look around.

You will never guess one of the things we loved about this hotel—it was the first one we visited that had an ice machine on the floor, or anywhere else for that matter! Ice was something I had really started to miss from home. As we approached our room, the hotel's feeling of grandeur was exciting, even as tired as we were.

Rvain O'Connor, the general manager, whom I didn't get the chance to meet, oversees a staff of 110 people. Prior to 2006, the hotel had been known as Jury's Cork Hotel for forty years. Today, The River Lee Hotel is a family owned, corporately held company—high quality, yet personal. At the River Lee, you find yourself wrapped in luxury and pampered as much as you allow yourself to be! There are 182 rooms, with mostly two double beds in each, but they do have the larger size beds you may request. There are many smaller hotels that close for the winter in Ireland due to a lack of business, but The River Lee stays open all year long. They also have fine dining available in the hotel with a seating capacity of 140 people, and they offer catering for groups up to sixty people.

One of the many highlights to enjoy at this property is the annual Jazz Festival in October.

I have two people at The River Lee Hotel to thank for the information and photos in this section: Claire Myler and Paula Cogan. Paula has been working with me to find an offer just for you. Her very special idea was to assign a code expression to the offer to make it unique, and this idea kick-started the other locations we visited around Ireland to do the same with their special offers. Paula's idea was to use the expression "The Gift of Gab," which is fitting for the River Lee area because Blarney Castle is nearby where the legend from this expression derives. Be sure to check out our website for the offers and see which other locations may have joined in with fun phrases! Thank you, Paula, for making our offers to our readers a fun event.

Although Paula says every guest is important to her and the hotel, she says they also have had celebrity guests like Roy Keane, a former Irish footballer and manager. Also, the very talented Jonathan Rhys Myers, a singer, musician, actor, and model who is best known for his role as Henry VIII in the TV series *The Tudors*.

Paula recommends that visitors to the hotel and Cork be sure not to miss the Honan Chapel and The Glucksman Gallery at University College of Cork (UCC). Let me give you some information about those properties.

Glucksman Gallery at UCC

According to the UCC website[1]:

"UCC ART COLLECTION University College Cork has over 350 works in its collection. These works are sited throughout the campus to provide the UCC community and visitors with a first-hand encounter with original works of art. The UCC Art Collection concentrates on contemporary Irish art and now features many of Ireland's most distinguished practitioners."

Second: Honan Chapel

Built in 1915, and named for the family that funded it, Honan Chapel is known for many things, among them the mosaic floor, the tabernacle, and special windows. It was blessed as sacred in November 1916, and became a gathering place for prayer at the UCC campus.

The River Lee is a sister property to The Westbury Hotel in Dublin. Both hotels have extended generous offers to our readers. Please visit our website at www.ExtraordinaryIreland.com for the most updated offers.

1 http://www.ucc.ie/en/

Paula Cogan's contact information is as follows: (will be repeated at the end)

Contact Information:
Paula Cogan, Director of Sales & Marketing
The River Lee Hotel
Email: paula_Cogan@doylecollection.com
Phone: 353 21 4937712

You can completely rely on Paula and Claire so we recommend that you contact them for reservations. They will be sure you are taken care of, and hey, why not be pampered by two of the best in the business? These executives care about your comfort.

I interviewed Paula by asking her many questions, so you can have an idea of who she is. I would like to share a few of her answers.

Paula, as Director of Sales and Marketing, is second in command at this huge property. That cannot be an easy task, but she does it with grace and willingness to tend to your happiness. She was born and raised in Cork City and has an appreciation for the finer sites you will want to visit. The following is a quote from her so words do not get scrambled:

"While I am slightly biased, as I was born and bred in Cork, the City has, and continues to have, an International outlook, be it the historic port of Cobh or the trading City that Cork has always been. Even today, Cork plays host to a selection of International companies, including many U.S. companies who have set up in Cork. As the old saying goes, we are the neighboring parish of Boston and the U.S.A."

Take your bathing suits, as you do not want to miss out on a swim in The River Lee's fabulous pool after a day of sightseeing!

Hint: If you do not book through the hotel directly, be sure to TAKE A COPY OF YOUR CONFIRMATION to prove you paid for whatever package you may have reserved. Example: special room or full Irish breakfast.

The restaurant is fairly upscale and the food is excellent.

Room Tip: Always go to the Doyle Collection for the best price. The Doyle Collection is the name of the hotel group that includes The River Lee. Look them up online at www.doylecollection.com to view all their properties.

Interesting Facts about Cork:

In 1917, Henry Ford opened a car factory in Cork called the Buttermarket. However, it closed down in 1924.

In 1963, President John F. Kennedy visited Cork.

The 1980s were hard times in Cork since many businesses such as the Dunlop Tire Factory, manufacturing companies, and many shipbuilding companies closed, leaving the city with high unemployment.

Cork began to rebound in the 1990s with new industries, a commercial park, and an airport business park. Today, the city employs people to work in chemicals, food processing, brewing, and more. You can find a lot of history in Cork and enjoy yourselves while learning about our neighbors!

Cork is Ireland's second-largest city and well-known for its lively nightlife and reasonably peaceful days, as well as good pubs, shopping, and a few annual festivals.

In 2010, Cork was named one of the Top 10 Cities in the World to visit by *Lonely Planet*. Steeped in history, Cork City is fast gaining a reputation as one of Europe's happening cities. Like Venice, the city is built on water, and the city center is built on an island in the River Lee, just upstream of Cork Harbor. The two channels of the River Lee, which embrace the city center, are spanned by many bridges and this gives the city a distinctive continental air.

There is so much history in this town. Just listing all the interesting facts would take much too long, so be sure you investigate on your own because exploring Cork and its many historical places is an enjoyable way to spend several days. You must see the Ring of the Shandon Bells in the 300 year-old tower of St. Anne's Church, and marvel at the French Gothic spires of St. Finbarre's Cathedral. You will discover unique shopping and dining options, among them the famous English Market, with its stalls selling foods from all over the world. The English Market allows you to stock your pantry for several days should you be renting a self-catering accommodation as a base location for exploring the area.

Among the "can't miss" sites to visit in Cork is the fabulous waterfront. Rich farmlands and river valleys contrast with the wild sandstone hills of the west. Cork is dubbed the Gourmet Capitol of Ireland, but the one sure treasure of Cork, as in the East and West Coastlines, are the beaches alongside the Atlantic Ocean that offer a strange peacefulness as they roar during a storm!

This city, like so many others in Ireland, is one you do not want to miss. Plan out your vacation so you know what there is to see, and so you do not waste precious time trying to make decisions on the spot. Because we planned everything out, our vacation was full from day to day. Be sure to save some unplanned time each day to allow for unexpected sites along the way!

THE ENGLISH MARKET

Visiting the English Market is a real experience. You will not soon forget it! We had mixed emotions and feelings at first, but it became clear we were seeing a slice of everyday life. The English Market is a grand place, but we did not understand why it was a tourist attraction.

The English Market seems to be referenced in every tourist book about Ireland, so it conjures up many thoughts in tourists' minds. The only problem is most of the books do not tell you it is an actual market, like your local grocery store, where you go to buy your fresh, everyday mealtime supplies. Some items, however, are unique to the English Market, and you will probably not find them in any other store around Ireland, or in your hometown either, for that matter. You might find something like it in Seattle's Pike Place Market, but even that isn't too close!

Since so many tour books told us to visit the English Market, we put it on our agenda. But what we really found there was surprising!

First, if you decide to go, parking is a nightmare, so plan on trying to find space in the parking garages. Plan to spend plenty of time at the Market because it is so crowded and busy it will take a while to see everything and make any purchases. We found only one pay toilet (there may have been more) for both men and women and it was busy, too! So if you take the children, you may want to locate the toilets before browsing the Market!

It is almost a shame that the English Market attracts tourists precisely because it is the locals' grocery market, so if you do not have a kitchen or plan in some way to buy food to cook, you are really getting in the way. The people of Cork are just trying to move through the English Market quickly so they can get supplies for their daily meals! However, if you do plan to buy food, bring along your backpack because you will end up wanting to buy everything!

We had a vacation rental in Kinsale with a fully equipped kitchen so we knew from the locals we had met that we would find meats, chicken, or fish at the English Market. That is why we went! We enjoyed the lunch meats, stuffed chicken breast, and pre-formed hamburger patties that were only a single Euro each, but we observed many gawkers who had no intentions of shopping! We were certainly no different since we were there because of the write-ups in tour books, too, but we also had a need and desire for fresh meats, vegetables, and fruits. Yes, we could have gone to a local market, but the locals told us the prices were much better at the English Market. Since we were in Cork, we decided to go.

If you are in Cork and think the English Market might be a good place for souvenirs, stay away! There are none. The restaurant everyone speaks of upstairs is the same. Everyone goes there because it is written about in the tour books. If you want an average meal in a busy, crowded, and noisy restaurant, by all means go there. But if you want a great meal and want to eat with the locals, may we suggest you try any of the other restaurants along the waterfront. Or try one of the pubs. Pubs throughout Ireland serve food and always seem to provide terrific meals at reasonable prices. And you can get to know the people at the tables next to you! Children are welcome in almost every pub while eating as long as they are accompanied by an adult. Or if you want to splurge a bit, try the fine dining at the River Lee Hotel.

The English Market is not a grand place, but it is essential for how many people live their lives day to day. We owe it to our neighbors not to intrude as lookie loos unless we are visiting actual tourist attractions such as castles. Take your family to another attraction because the English Market has nothing for the tourist who is just traveling through!

There are no crafts or handmade goods, nor even a place where children can be. Do not expect to find soda or slurpees there either. Of course, if you are looking for awesome breads or cheeses to snack on while driving along the highways, look no further because they have them at the English Market. But the chocolate store was definitely a disappointment; what we found there were small, tiny overpriced pieces, many of which did not even come from Ireland!

Now, I do not mean to give you negative comments about this wonderful market; I just want you to know that it is everyday life for the local people and not a playground. You probably could not want for anything fresher for a food selection than what you will find there, for both basic and even expanded needs in a kitchen. We did, however, hear a few comments from the vendors that they wished people who did not have business there would let the ones who did get closer to the counters so their business could carry on.

Whether you visit the English Market or not, as I said, you don't want to miss the town of Cork. And by all means, if you are in need of anything that can be found at the market, you will find a huge assortment of it. Visit there and enjoy!

Chapter 6

KINSALE

Kinsale is a small, quaint, and charming fishing town in County Cork of about three thousand people. It is known for its quiet scenery and a lush green landscape, but it also has a busy harbor buzzing with activity. Kinsale's restaurants are known  for their food and award-winning menus. We were also told about a local festival in October each year for four days called the Gourmet Festival. The tourist information center told me that it attracts residents from all over Ireland filling the streets with several hundred visitors.

When we arrived in Kinsale, we tucked into a restaurant along the harbor side to warm up and have a small lunch. We ordered the vegetable soup, and much to our surprise, here again was a soup where no vegetables could be seen! It was amazing—there were no visible vegetables in any of the soups we ordered throughout the isle. The veggies were there, of course. They pureed them. All the soups are creamy…and delightful!

Kinsale is loaded with shops that support local artists and area craftspeople. You can find just about anything you would want to find in Kinsale. The town is inviting and full of character—colorful window dressings, flower boxes and friendly people. Be sure to visit Granny's Bottom Drawer. This small shop had everything you could want—Traditional Irish Linens and lace, a full stock of tablecloths, pillowcases, table runners and hand-

This photo was taken from our car as we searched for a parking space, which did not exist, at least not near anyplace we wanted to go!

crocheted placemats, which we bought our fair share of! As I have mentioned before, be sure to save all your receipts or you will be held responsible for the 21 percent sales tax.

Kinsale has many other activities for those looking for a restful visit to a beautiful little town, including an organized walking tour, water sports, whale and dolphin watching tours, and golfing. But since word has gotten out about the town's attractions, tourists flock there in droves, making this is a busy little town. Definitely make reservations before you get there!

Since the town is so popular, you also have to be careful because traffic is heavy, and as in much of Ireland, the streets are very narrow so you need to be watchful. Our apartment attached to our landlord's residence was on a hairpin road that was interesting for us to navigate!

We selected this small community to use for our base camp, but we're not sure that was the best choice. Kinsale is definitely a town you want to visit, but it might be a bit too far south for a base camp. If you are going to look for a base location for this area, may we suggest you either stay in Blarney or Cork, which are more centrally located for sightseeing trips, offering shorter drives and easier and quicker access to primary roads and attractions. Still, Kinsale is only about a thirty-minute drive from Cork, so you be the judge. It's a choice between privacy or convenience. It's up to you.

PISCES APARTMENT

All that being said, we want to tell you about our stay in Kinsale. We stayed in a self-catering apartment there called "Pisces Apartment" and the location was truly beautiful.

Contact Information:	
Irene Jones	
Email:	Pandijones@eircom.net
Phone:	021 4777750
Address:	Pisces Scilly
	Kinsale, Co Cork, Ireland

Irene was our hostess and you couldn't ask for a better landlady. She had lost her husband three weeks before we arrived, yet she graciously greeted us and made us feel at home. This is a home away from home! The apartment is connected to the main home,  but very private. Irene even invited us to sit on her patio to watch the boats go by.

In this two bedroom apartment, you will find a washer/dryer, complete kitchen with eating bar, two bathrooms, a small dining area, and a roomy living room with television. The apartment was well decorated and very clean. It is fully equipped with everything you need, as well as some basic pantry foods. The refrigerator is ample for your daily needs. This property is perfect for those who enjoy their privacy and want a view worth a million dollars!

The ocean harbor inlet was right outside our window so we could see across the Sound. It was definitely a busy port; we watched as the Customs boats buzzed the area daily. We were told they protect the shores from anyone trying to smuggle drugs into the country.

CUSTAIM (Customs Boat)

Our apartment was close to dining and everything in Kinsale. We only used one bedroom, but used the other room for our luggage. The apartment can easily accommodate a family of four or two couples. The cost is comparable to the local hotels, but here you can enjoy your own kitchen and do your wash before moving on! Your privacy is protected and no one bothers you for anything. Irene has even collected a portfolio for the local and not so local tours and other things to do in the area that she left for us to view. We learned many interesting facts about the area from this information, including that the part of Kinsale we were staying in is actually called Scilly.

The only negatives were the decidedly handicapped-unfriendly flight of stairs and the small showers. Otherwise, it is the absolutely perfect apartment or lodging in Kinsale. FYI: We stayed for the entire week since that is the way this apartment is rented.

Irene is a joy to have as a landlady and one of the kindest people you will ever know. Thank you, Irene, for sharing your lovely home with us.

If you visit Kinsale, please say hello to Irene from Doug and Rosemary!

Across the street from our apartment was The Spaniard, a local pub with a grand restaurant menu. We thoroughly enjoyed our time there!

We walked through the town many times either to shop, take a tour, have dinner, shop for fresh fish to cook at our apartment, or sit by the waterside!

We took boat tours to James Fort and Charles Fort. We saw the forts strictly by water, but this also allowed us to see so many beautiful areas we may have missed otherwise. If you take these types of trips, we want to warn you it is not warm in Ireland most of the time, so take a scarf or sweater with you. Umbrellas are always a good idea as well!

I, loving to shop, found many fine places of interest, including a linen store with all the bargains a larger city would have to offer, but an even nicer selection. The mentality of this town, again, is much the same as it is in all of Ireland—if they think you look lost, they stop you and ask if you are okay, or if they can help you! How wonderful it is to be so welcome in a foreign land, or anywhere for that matter!

We planned to stay for the week, but left a day early for another town where a tour had been booked. Still, we definitely enjoyed our stay in Kinsale.

KINSALE HARBOR TRIP: FORTS AND LIGHTHOUSE

On this trip we experienced cloudy skies and a heavy dew, but by the time we sailed, it was nice again.

Note: Don't let Ireland's weather stop you from doing what you think you will enjoy, as the "four seasons in a day" happens almost every day!

The scenery was breathtaking as we sailed out past the hundreds of boats in the Kinsale Marina. The sea-going commercial vessels were huge and offered an interesting view like none we had ever seen.

Jerome, owner of the "Spirit of Kinsale Harbour Cruise," gives you a commentary full of information, so you can learn about the historical sites you will see. But beware; sit where you can hear him. If the boat is crowded and everyone decides to talk, hearing can be a challenge! He tells you a bit of the history of how Kinsale grew up through the centuries and even throws in a legend or two along the way to spice things up.

Above: View Kinsale from the water with Kinsale Harbour Cruises and see the area like you couldn't any other way. (www.kinsaleharbourcruises.com)

Bottom: One of the nearby Forts

You'll have a chance to view sea life, plant growth, and sights of the town as you cruise along the edge of the Marina and pass into the Sound.

You will have the opportunity to see Charles Fort, built in the late 1600s to reinforce the harbor's defenses. This fort was built stone by stone. Let your imagination take you there so you can appreciate what they must have gone through to build and protect this area. At one time, this fort had a garrison, but after 1920 and the War of Independence, it was surrendered to the Free State Government and is now a heritage site with daily guided tours.

James Fort, on the opposite side of the harbor's mouth, was built in 1603, following the Battle of Kinsale, to prevent any further invasion and to secure the harbor. There are clear views of The Old Head of Kinsale before you turn at the mouth of the harbor.

With your imagination's ability to take you back in time, you could well feel the history and power of these two forts and understand the role they played in the defense of Kinsale.

Just beyond is the Block House, built in 1549, to store ammunition. You then sail past Ringrone Castle, built in the thirteenth century. The castle was vacated in the seventeenth century.

With a maximum of fifty passengers, the boat is designed with groups  in mind and can be reserved for private sailing. If you have a larger group, the cruises offer many specials. Refreshments are available, as are the all important bathroom facilities, which I was certainly happy to know!

Your captain and narrator, Jerome Lordan, was a fisherman for twenty-eight years and grew up in the area of Kinsale. He took over the *Spirit of Kinsale* in May 2005. The boat is locally owned and has been operated by Jerome for the last seven years.

The *Spirit of Kinsale* also has a range of beverages available on board for passengers to enjoy while taking in the scenery, or while reading some of the literature downstairs.

Enjoy this part of your trip by relaxing and learning. It's worth your time!

Tips: You can visit the Charles Fort, but it is sometimes closed due to bad weather, so check the schedules.

Lastly, when I asked the *Spirit*'s crew who their most important guest had been, the reply was, "We like to treat our passengers equally, to make them as comfortable and as informed as possible, whether they are celebrities or not. We don't differentiate and believe it is unprofessional to do so."

According to Jerome, "As well as having a thirst for archeology and local history (including the many shipwrecks), and having a wide knowledge of seafaring after fishing and skippering for many years, I am very passionate about preserving the old Irish place-names of local areas as they provide a window into the past and of the lives of the people who used them." Jerome also offers a two- to three-hour FREE historical walking tour of the Old Head of Kinsale once a year during the Ballinspittle festival, in July.

Kinsale Harbour Cruises	
Email:	harbourcruises@gmail.com
Website:	www.kinsaleharbourcruises.com
Telephone:	+353 86 2505456
Harbour Cruise Prices:	Adult: €12.50
	Children (Under 14): €6.00
	Children (Under 2): Free
	Family Rate (2A + 2C): €32.00
	Group Rate (More): €10.50
	Kids free (1 per adult, Mon—Fri)
	The math is approximately the Euro times 1.5 for the US dollar figure. Be sure to check for up-to-date information before you go.

THE SPANIARD: PUB AND RESTAURANT

You also want to be sure to visit The Spaniard Inn. The Spaniard is one of the oldest pubs in the area and certainly has character. It was built on the site of a ruined castle around 1650, and was called the Castle Bar. In those days, it was run by the Coleman Family.

The establishment became quite famous as a place for sailors and fishermen to hang out while away from home. It was later renamed for Don Juan d'Aquila, a Spanish Naval commander, who became a local hero fighting alongside the Irish in 1601 at the Battle of Kinsale.

The current owners, David Shaw and Mary O'Dwyer, have made sure that tradition is honored and have kept the fine dining menu and welcoming bar they inherited when they purchased the restaurant. In 2004, the Spaniard won the Traditional Irish Music Award and recently added the Georgina Campbell/Jameson Whiskey Award.

The Spaniard Inn's outer walls are picturesque and the pub sports a thatched roof. On the inside, you will find the lights down low to create a lively atmosphere with seating at tables, the bar, or a small area by the fireplace, which warms the main room. Most nights The Spaniard offers live music from Traditional to Russian Gypsy later in the evenings and a dinner menu that we enjoyed very much.

DRIVE FROM KINSALE TO MIZEN HEAD

If you are in a rental car, take off and be adventuresome! We set out from Kinsale early in the morning for a very long day traveling to Mizen Head. (The trip would have been easier from Cork, which is what I meant about staying in Cork as a base camp, but the trade off is missing this wonderful place.) We took a different route on our return trip and saw some amazing sites!

May I suggest packing a small overnight bag when exploring in case you find a place along the way you simply want to stay and explore for the night! We took off early and did not return until eleven hours later, but we would have been less tired had

we stopped and stayed at the amazing place we found near Mizen Head!

There are so many wonderful places along the way that we would never finish this section of the book if we listed them all, so we will just talk about a few.

KANTURK CASTLE

We travelled through an area where the Kanturk Castle remains in ruins. There is some dispute as to whether the castle was built for MacDonogh MacCarthy or Dermot MacOwen.

Heck, not even the actual construction date can be agreed upon or determined, but it is believed the castle was built in the late sixteenth or early seventeenth century.

I read that the neighbors watching this huge castle being built worried about the owner's intentions and asked the Queen to intervene. The Queen ordered construction stopped. (It is said, "If a Man's Castle is his home, then it is no longer his when the

Doug and Rosemary at Kanturk Castle

Queen arrives!") Before construction was halted the castle's four-story main structure and towers were completed.

Four hundred years later, the castle still stands strong for all to see and it is worth the stop. You may wonder what it was about this castle that worried the neighbors but that question will remain a mystery.

Down through time, the property has changed hands many times, and since July 2000, it has been managed by The National Trust for Ireland. Who knows? Maybe you could buy this castle and finish building it yourself!

Road to Rosscarberry

Take a break before traveling down some very narrow roads that will truly make your stomach turn; I think it is the eyes that make you nervous. On some roads there's barely room for one car, but it is a two way road anyway!

ROSSCARBERY

The above picture is of the first view we saw as we arrived in Rosscarberry. We're sure you will also find charm in all the history here. Several famous people call Rosscarberry home, including O'Donovan Rossa, a Fenian (freeholder/warrior) and manager of the Irish people; Thomas Barry, prominent guerrilla leader in the Irish Republican Army; and Michael Collins, an Irish Revolutionary leader. Enjoy your time in Rosscarberry and remember you can find many nice gifts in this small town, not to mention the memories you will carry home.

Upon our arrival, Rosscarberry was sparkling like a diamond, as you can see in the picture above! It was so nice to see a road that did not cross my eyes trying to see the other lane.

And what a surprise when we stopped at a market and I ran into someone there talking town history. He told me the churches in town were special because this town was blessed and known as a Cathedral town! Now, I was not sure whether he was teasing me, but it did have a few spectacular churches and a Cathedral that was truly amazing, so I chose to believe him. I have since confirmed his story on the Internet. In fact, Rosscarbery is home to one of Ireland's smallest cathedrals, St. Fachtna.

Rosscarbery is a small town cradled on a hillside overlooking an inlet on the West Cork coastline. The town center is set up with visitors in mind, and you will find plenty of places to stay for however long you decide while you explore the regions of Cork and Kerry. This town offers visitor shopping, parks where you can pack a picnic lunch and enjoy the surroundings of the Castlefreke Castle, and beaches to walk along.

When we arrived, there was a peaceful, yet sophisticated feel about the town. However, you will still find the busy pubs with their live entertainment to while away the day. Be sure to catch the Saturday morning traditional farmers market for local produce. Want to be spoiled? Try one of the several gourmet restaurants.

MIZEN PENINSULA:
ALTAR WEDGE TOMB

This tomb is situated on the side of R 592, just over four miles west of Skull on a level plat about ten feet off the road and about 100 feet from the ocean shoreline. It is one of many tombs on the Mizen Peninsula. Just beyond the tomb you can see Toormore Bay.

In 1989, when the tomb was excavated by Dr. William O'Brien and Madeline Duggan, a small deposit of fish bones, seashells, and human remains were found. The following information is copied from a sign I photographed at the site:

"Built from local slabs, this wedge shaped tomb is one of a dozen in the Mizen Peninsula. It was first erected at the end of the stone age, about 3,000 to 2,000 BC, with its entrance deliberately lined up with the Mizen Peak. Archaeologists recently uncovered some burnt human bone which they radiocarbon dated about to 2,000 BC and believe that the tomb continued to be used as a sacred site in the centuries to follow.

The ritual use of this site ended with Christianity, but it was briefly resumed during the eighteenth century when the tomb was used for an altar by priests who were forbidden by law to say Mass in a church."

Photo taken from our car while we followed behind a truck! If you look, you will see that his wheels are partly on the other side of the road!

MIZEN HEAD

Oh my! Here we are again on these wonderfully maintained, but awfully narrow roads. We wondered how oncoming cars could possible get by us! Thank goodness there are at least lovely purple wildflowers everywhere to see. They distract your eyes from these narrow roads.

Mizen Head (in Irish: Carn Ui Neid) is located at the extreme western end of a peninsula where the Atlantic roars against the coastline and is reportedly the most southwestern point of Ireland in West County Cork. I say reportedly because although the Mizen Head visitor center makes the claim, other sources claim Brow Head holds that distinction. So which is it?

From the visitors station (center) you can stand by the fenced area on the cliff-side and take some photographs that are truly outstanding. Here you will also find an old signaling station, a weather station, and a lighthouse.

FINALLY HERE!

These high cliffs are a spectacular location and will give you the feeling you have reached heaven. From this vantage point you may spot whales, dolphins, seals, and a variety of birds. If you are ambitious, you can take the stroll across the ninety-nine steps and across the arched bridge to visit the signal station. Many distinctions are attributed to the Mizen Head Signal Station, including the station being the first to receive a Radio Beacon in Ireland in 1931. You will also enjoy the gift shop and cafe. We found many postcards to send home and enjoyed a soup and sandwich lunch.

Mizen Head View

This place took my breath away! And probably will do the same for you. There is a quiet peacefulness at the ocean side here during a storm, and if you are fortunate enough to be here when the rain stops, the rainbow over the sea may be one of the most inspiring sights you'll ever see.

This trip, although long, was an amazing journey. We met some fine people, saw sites we never knew existed, observed farmers in the field, and saw rolls of turf (peat) used for both fires and oven baking! At least the farmers have an energy source to help them manage and it's too bad we in the United States don't consider how efficient it seems to be.

On the way back to Kinsale from Mizen Head, I was not feeling really grand. We had had a long day and were tired and my stomach was upset.

We came upon a hotel called Barley Cove Beach Hotel. We needed to use its facilities and I needed to wash my face. The owner there, Mark, was most obliging and allowed me the use of his lobby restroom. Afterwards, we talked about his absolutely beautiful hotel, and believe me, this is a go to destination. If you can arrange it, spend a couple of days here just to relax and enjoy the peacefulness around you. The beach walks and spending time at Mizen Head make this the hotel for you.

Chapter 7

BLARNEY CASTLE

"Blarney!" That's the word. This special castle was responsible for bringing the word Blarney into our language, and it's so much fun to use. And wait until you see the photo to follow that shows the height of where you need to climb to gain the Gift of

Gab! The famous Blarney Stone is 85 feet up from the ground!

This castle was built in 1446, but all that remains is the tower where the famous Blarney Stone is found. Many tourists are drawn to this location to gain the special gift said to be bestowed if you hang upside down to kiss the rock. Hint: "Empty your pockets first." That was the advice I was given! Also, I observed many tourists tipping as I had read in other travel books, but the one thing those books had said was that people customarily tipped after they kissed the stone, but I think you may be wise to tip them beforehand!

Blarney Castle Tower

Now I know you must be thinking, "Who wants to kiss a stone?" but luck is with all those who do and there is plenty of support holding your legs as

"Kissing the Blarney Stone"

you lay upside down over a long drop to the ground. Photos are also taken so you can show them to all your friends.

Blarney is located about five miles from Cork City and reachable by car or bus. The stories vary about the Blarney Stone, but truth be known, no one seems to know for sure the actual story of where this stone comes from or how it actually came to be the most famous rock in Ireland!

A bit of history I was able to find from Blarney Castle about its origins and the stone go like this:

Blarney Castle was originally constructed of wood in the tenth century. Around 1210 AD, it was replaced by a stone structure with an entrance on the North Face, twenty some feet above the ground. It was demolished and a third castle was built in 1446, leaving the remains we see today.

Now we come to the story regarding the famous Blarney Stone! Blarney Castle was occupied by the King of Munster who sent four thousand soldiers from Munster to Robert the Bruce in Scotland in 1314 to fight the English. According to legend (found or reported by Blarney Castle historians), Robert the Bruce gave the King of Munster half of Scotland's sacred Stone of Scone in gratitude. This half of the Stone of Scone is known as the Blarney Stone and it was placed in the battlements where it is now seen by millions and can be kissed!

In the sixteenth century, Queen Elizabeth I commanded the Earl of Leicester to take possession of the castle, but when he tried to speak with the Irish Lord of Blarney, McCarthy, he was always side-tracked with talk of banquets. When the Earl was asked for progress reports, there were none except long messages that the castle had still not been taken. The delays caused Queen Elizabeth to become irritated and she remarked that the Earl's reports were "nothing but Blarney!" That was how a new word was introduced to the English language! I have seen this story on the literature at the castle, so I tend to believe it.

Another story claims that in the 1830s a Father Prout may have given magical powers to the Stone when he declared that whoever kisses it shall gain eloquence! Now which tale do you believe? No matter, millions of people visit this castle to enjoy a peaceful day on the grounds and see what all the myths or truths are all about.

During the English Civil War in the mid-seventeenth century, Oliver Cromwell's General, Lord Broghill, succeeded in breaking the castle walls, but when he did, he discovered that the main garrison had escaped in the underground caves where there were three routes that would take them either to Cork, the Lake, or Kerry, and reportedly they had taken the gold plate with them.

The castle continued to belong to the McCarthy family until Donogh Mc-Carthy, 4th Earl of Clancarthy, passed it over to the Hollow Sword Blade Company who subsequently sold it in 1688, to Sir James St. John Jefferyes, the Governor of Cork. That same year, the lake was drained in an effort to find the gold plate but it was never found.

According to the Blarney Castle website:[1]

"At the beginning of the eighteenth century during the reign of Queen Anne, Sir James St. John Jefferyes built a Georgian gothic house up against the keep of the castle as was then the custom all over Ireland. At the same time the Jefferyes family laid out a landscape garden known as the Rock Close with a remarkable collection of massive boulders and rocks arranged around what seemed to have been druid remains from pre-historic times.

"In 1820, the house was accidentally destroyed by fire and the wings now form a picturesque adjunct to the keep, recently in the 1980s, rearranged to give a better view of the keep. The Jefferyes intermarried on 14th January 1846, with the Colthurst family of Ardrum, Inniscarra and Ballyvourney, Co. Cork, and Lucan, Co. Dublin. The early children dying, Lady Colthurst decided to build the new castle in Scottish baronial style south of

1 http://www.blarneycastle.ie/pages/history

the present location. This was completed in 1874, and has been the family home ever since."

We would like to thank the staff at Blarney Castle for the information and photographs in this chapter.

We found the photos below to be of special interest. They were provided to us for your enjoyment by Blarney Castle, as was the text that is with the photos.

Blarney Castle

"In bygone years, fern seeds were thought to make one invisible. They allow the finder to understand the language of birds, find buried treasures, and have the strength of forty men. As ever at Blarney, exploration is rewarded. Where one can become Invisible!"

"The Witch's Stone" *Blarney Castle*

"It takes little imagination to see who is imprisoned here. The Witch of Blarney has been with us since the dawn of time. Some say it was she who first told McCarthy of the power of the Blarney Stone. Fortunately for visitors, she only escapes the witch stone after nightfall—and we close at dusk."

That story makes you wonder what else may lurk on this land!

The website also states that the castle is now available to be used in films:

"Within a short drive of Cork International Airport, we can offer a wide range of architectural styles and many different landscapes. Despite our long history and world renowned natural beauty, the Estate has only been made available for filming on rare occasions in the past. With the improvements of recent years, we believe we can now offer film makers a secure and full facility."

While we were here, we were told people had taken rocks from the castle and then claimed they had had the worst luck while the stones were in their possession. There is a sign asking you not to take any rocks from the property. The staff told us that some of those people had reportedly returned the rocks through the mail and later reported their luck had gotten much better!

It is worth the time to look around and enjoy the grounds if you are looking for a quiet day. You will find the staff to be most helpful.

Contact Information

Email:	info@blarneycastle.ie
Website:	http://www.blarneycastle.ie/pages/contact
Telephone:	00 353 21 438 5252
Opening Times:	Open All Year Round!

Monday to Saturday

May: 9:00 a.m. to 6:30 p.m.
Jun-Jul-Aug: 9:00 a.m. to 7:00 p.m.
Sept: 9:00 a.m. to 6:30 p.m.
Oct-Apr: 9:00 a.m. to sundown

Sundays

Summer: 9:00 a.m. to 5:30 p.m.
Winter: 9:00 a.m. to sundown
Last Admissions is 30 minutes before closing.
The Castle, Rock Close Gardens, and Lakeland Walk are open all year, except Christmas Eve and Christmas Day.

Blarney Castle Visitor Rates	Adult Admission: €10
	Students / Seniors: €8
	Children (8-14 years): €3.50
	Family (2 Adults, 2 Children): €23.50

Guidebooks are available in French, English, and German.

Wedding Parties	Please contact the office at 021-4385252 for access to the Castle for the purpose of Wedding Photography.

"Dublin House and Castle"

Sources for this story and some photographs:

Thank you, Blarney Castle, for text used directly from your materials on your website and photographs provided for reprint and by permission.

Chapter 8

BLARNEY WOOLLEN MILLS
The Legend

While in Ireland, we experienced sun and rain and on the very same day, the wind would kick up, causing you to be chilled enough to wear winter sweaters. Another excuse to shop the sweater mills! Blarney Woolen Mills is especially fun to visit. One can enter the warm decor and friendliness

This is one of the most exciting places to shop, eat, and stay!

and shop till you drop! Or not! I myself fell in love with the hats, scarves, linen, crystal, pottery, key chains, postcards, jewelry (you can also find the Claddagh ring here as well), t-shirts, and sweatshirts—not to mention the Irish Linen nightshirts or gowns. And that is only the beginning.

A great cup of tea or coffee with perhaps a fresh baked scone gets you going again, so you can shop again before lunch! Blarney is a grand location. Do not plan on just one day here since you'll want time to visit Blarney Castle and the Woollen Mills.

Please believe me, we do not work for, have not been commissioned by, nor are we associated with this or any other mill in Ireland or elsewhere. We just wish to share our honest opinion about this fine store and share a little of our experiences there before we present the store's history.

When we first arrived in Blarney, we had an appointment at Blarney Castle to interview some of the staff for our book. At the end of that visit, they asked if we had gone to the Woollen Mills yet and said they would call ahead and make arrangements for us to interview people there as well. With excitement in our hearts, we gratefully accepted the offer. We had not known who to contact at the mill, but now we had the perfect solution to bring an interesting story to our readers. Thank you, Jean Murphy at Blarney Castle, for helping us. Jean told us the man who was going to meet us had said to look for the good looking, kind man in the pin stripe suit! He was just kidding around, but this kind man, Darren Smyth, was exactly that! He graciously gave of himself on short notice and allowed us all the time we needed.

We were taken on a tour that was priceless. We began outside in the parking lot where a small thatched roof building was erected and standing on the edge of this huge lot. It was the original souvenir shop that existed there, but had later moved inside the mill which had been converted to a hotel.

We enjoyed every moment there and were treated as though we were family. When we arrived, I asked about the history of the Woollen Mills. Darren took us on a tour and explained the history of the mill and the dream of the ambitious person who created the Blarney Woollen Mills! And despite this store doing a great business, you could not find a more caring staff, which speaks well of the company altogether.

We wanted more than just to shop. We wanted a place that could handle anything we would need or want to take home. Even though it was June, it was very cold in Ireland, so we needed sweaters. As luck would have it, there was a sale on while we were there. We bought six sweaters, which took care of some of our Christmas shopping and allowed us to share part of our trip with friends and loved ones. We wanted to take home gifts, too, for our travel agent, business associates, and so many others. We found it all here. Sweaters, hats, scarves, all made with the finest wool. We found Waterford Crystal, postcards to send home, key chains, t-shirts, shot glasses, lovely Irish Linen, and the list goes on!

You can even take a break in the attached restaurant and enjoy a marvelous lunch or dinner with a wide range of choices, or dine in a more private restaurant on the same property.

We did not stay at the Blarney Woolen Mills Hotel because we did not know about it when we were planning our trip. But now that we've seen what is there, I promise one thing—our return trip will include this location as our base for travel around the immediate area.

BLARNEY WOOLEN MILLS HOTEL

After returning home and handing out our gifts, many asked me to order them other items. Although the mill has a website, some items were not listed, so I wrote to ask about them. The

A typical room at the hotel

staff went out of its way to process my orders without ever complaining. Our order was handled with no issues. It was timely, compassionate to our needs, and very helpful no matter what we asked. We have never received this type of service from a retailer anywhere else in the world. The staff is so friendly they make you want to travel all the way back to Ireland just to shop. You do not have to take our word for it; just visit their website at www.blarney.com and look around—if you need anything, you can email them and ask. It is just that easy.

The woolen sweaters are an item you certainly must take home!

Say hello to Geraldine—the "go to" person for help

Playing at Blarney Woollen Mills with Hats!

While there, remember we told you many other items of interest can also be found. Thank you Blarney Woollen Mills, Darren, and Geraldine, for a job done with so much interest! We will be back!

But now, what would a shopping trip be in Ireland without a stop off at the neighborhood pub? Right again! Christy's Pub is right there on the property and chances are your husband has already found his way there while you were shopping.

One of the more interesting facts about Blarney Mills is that they are 100 percent Irish owned, producing fine wools and tweeds since 1823, although their mill is no longer in operation.

Darren told us, "Today we not only sell the best of Irish knitwear, but we also stock Waterford Crystal, Belleek China, Galway Crystal, Irish Linen and Lace, Celtic Jewellery, and much more."

Here are just a few of the facts about the history of this phenomenal place. Although begun in 1823, the mill closed down in 1973. Christy Kelleher then decided that he wanted to buy the mill and put people back to work so they could earn a living again and feed their families. He did not have the money, so he built a small, thatched roof building on wheels which became the beginning of his dream. Christy was a loving man who cared about the future of Blarney and the people who lived there. He himself had little other than his drive to succeed and a DREAM. The small, thatched roof building is still on the edge of the parking lot serving as a reminder of the mill's humble rebirth so many years ago.

Today, you will find Christy's daughter Freda's automobile parked just in front since Freda still runs the Blarney Woollen Mills and is very active in day-to-day operations. You can see her working as she visits around the store.

The following is from the Management of Blarney Woollen Mills.

THE STORY OF BLARNEY WOOLLEN MILLS

Cead Míle Fáilte—a hundred thousand welcomes to the charming little village of Blarney and to Blarney Woollen Mills. Nestled in the breathtaking scenery, the village, with its traditional square, lies in the shadow of Blarney Castle, home of the Blarney Stone. Legend has it that whoever kisses the stone will be endowed with the gift of eloquence.

"There is a stone that whoever kisses,

Oh! He never misses to grow Eloquent

'Tis he may clamber to a lady's chamber,

Or become a member of parliament."

Right in the heart of Blarney you will find Blarney Woollen Mills. Over the years the Kelleher family has taken great care to convert these huge rambling old Mill buildings into one of the world's greatest gift and craft centers. Millions of visitors have passed

Darren Smyth

through these doors from all over the world to be greeted with a warm Irish welcome and the very best of Irish products. Products that have been created by the finest craftsmen and women throughout the country, whose skills may be measured, not in decades, but in countless generations.

The name Blarney Woollen Mills has become synonymous with quality Irish products including our world famous hand knit sweaters made in Ireland.

We will introduce you to a new experience incorporating the unique village atmosphere which developed in Blarney largely because of the Woollen Mills, the historic castle and Christy Kelleher whose great vision started it all.

We hope you will agree that the atmosphere created here will leave you with a lasting and a pleasant memory of your visit to Blarney.

THE STORY

The earliest record of a castle in Blarney goes back to the year 1200, when the first stone structure was built on the site of the present castle. This was the seat of the McCarthy's, the great and noble kings of Munster, who, in 1446, extended the building along the lines familiar to us today. The original buildings covered some eight acres of land and catered not only for the McCarthy's, but for a huge retinue of knights and retainers. The castle was adjoined by a buttery, blacksmith's forge, stables and a mill for grinding corn.

By the year 1600, under the patronage of the McCarthy's, the Bardic School at Blarney had become legendary, attracting scholars from throughout Ireland, and Blarney's reputation as a place of learning, culture and poetry, developed. Within the castle walls, the McCarthy's always had a Bard in residence who served them as a poet, historian and musician.

The McCarthy's reigned throughout the troubled political period when Elizabeth I was attempting to force the Irish chieftains into submission. Outraged by the deft political maneuverings of Cormac McCarthy, Lord of Blarney, who did everything but submit, the British Queen, on receiving yet another flattering letter from the Munster King, is said to have shouted "This is all Blarney." Thus the term "Blarney," the ability to cajole with flattery entered the English language.

The McCarthy's suffered many an upheaval throughout this difficult period of Irish history, but after the battle of the Boyne in 1689, Prince William of Orange set about destroying the power of Irish chiefs once and for all, and the proud family was forced to leave Blarney Castle, never to return. The greatest of the McCarthy chieftains of the time, the Earl of Clancarthy, spent the remainder of his days exiled in Hamburg.

The Blarney property was then auctioned in the Tower of London and was eventually acquired by Sir James Jefferys, Governor of Cork, whose son, James St. John Jefferys, was responsible for developing Blarney Castle as we know it. Jefferys was also responsible for bringing the textile industry to the village, and by 1776, it was recorded that Blarney had 16 mills in all.

In the year 1741, Timothy Mahony, a wealthy landowner in County Kerry was faced with a problem common to many people living in Ireland at the time, one that effected a complete change in their way of living—under Penal Laws their land was confiscated and they were evicted. But Timothy was an innovative and resourceful man and rather than totally lose his self respect he decided to take the road to Cork and seek a new life. He saw a future in textiles and set up a small woollen mill in Cork in 1750. The company eventually settled in Blarney in a site "as picturesquely beautiful as could ever be found for the location of an industry."

The Blarney Mill was opened in 1824, by Timothy Mahony's grandson Martin and named Martin Mahony & Bros. Ltd. By 1835, it is recorded that 120 people worked at the mill, this rose to 200 by 1860, and most were housed in the new housing Millstream Row, smart modern housing built for the workers by the Mahonys.

Water was the power source for this expanding mill and the Mahonys went to considerable lengths to develop the abundant source. A large dam was built on the Martin River near Waterloo in order to form a mill pond. This gave the additional pressure required to drive the huge Millwheel at Blarney via the Millstream and Millrace.

During the mid 1800's, the devastating famine swept through Ireland. This was caused by the failure of the potato crop, Ireland's staple diet, and was responsible for the loss of three million souls, almost half the population. In Blarney, however, there were no recorded deaths by starvation during this period. The Mahonys were responsible for the employment of many desperate people during the famine which greatly helped the village survive this period of extreme hardship.

With the fullest co-operation of a grateful workforce, Martin Mahony and Bros. thrived during this time, producing serges and tweeds of an extremely high quality and competing successfully with English and Scottish counterparts.

The "bard of the Lee," Mr. John Fitzgerald, wrote in 1865: "with regard to the ancient industries of linen, cotton and paper, the millwheels turn not round with one very important exception, the Blarney Mills, where world famed Blarney Tweeds are made, and the establishment is still in the great Catholic hands of Mahony. This mill flourishes and gives employment to very many persons in the spinning, weaving and dyeing."

However, on a December night in 1869, disaster struck, and the Mill at Blarney was totally destroyed by fire. Daylight revealed a century's achievement reduced to nothing—a bitter blow to the people of Blarney who had come to rely on the mill as their means of livelihood, and a heartbreaking sight for the Mahony family.

But defeat was never considered and all the village's resources combined to clear away the debris and begin reconstruction of the fine building of Blarney Mills, some of which you can see today.

Again with much hard work on behalf of the Mahony family and the people of Blarney the mill prospered further and employment peaked at an all time high of 800 at the turn of the century. The Mahonys developed their own special materials which won many awards in international competition. Major extensions were made to the mill to cater for the latest production equipment which in the early 1900's, was said to have included 1,400 power looms, 13,000 spindles producing woollen and worsted cloths, tweeds, knitting wools and hosiery.

In 1928, a boy of thirteen, like most of his friends in Blarney, began to work at the mill. His name was Christy Kelleher.

Young Christy began work at the mill as an apprentice machinist and worked there for twenty-two years. During these formative and impressionable years Christy developed a great knowledge and awareness of the textile industry—qualities that would be put to good use in later years.

He became a supervisor with responsibility for the day to day running and maintenance of the heavy industrial machinery and was always very proud of the fact that during the war years when machine parts were not available, he improvised so well that "his" machines never stopped.

Nevertheless in 1951, Christy Kelleher left Mahony's to work with an insurance company in the city so that he could provide better for his family. He was never a man to sit still and always had a few additional "irons in the fire."

A succession of small businesses in the early years supplemented the family income. He took the local harrier club members to their drag hunts around Munster and operated a hackney service to bring the cycling club to their various meetings—for a modest fee! He ran a vegetable round on Saturday mornings and every Summer the entire family helped to harvest the orchard for which he had courageously "struck a price" the previous December.

As he got older the entrepreneur in Christy developed further. He purchased the local cinema—this was a dual purpose investment as it functioned as a cinema midweek and a dancehall at the weekends and all the family were roped in to help.

Above all, Christy was a passionate son of Blarney. He loved the village and its people and was proud of his Blarney roots.

Every Summer Christy watched as thousands of visitors came to Blarney, disembarked from their coaches, kissed the Blarney Stone and left

Blarney to go to their next destination. He knew that there should be other things of interest in Blarney if the visitors were to stay longer.

It was inevitable that Christy would start a venture that would ultimately benefit the village, and in 1967, because he did not have sufficient money to rent a shop, he built a small thatched cottage, on wheels, to sell crafts to the tourists. Freda, his eldest daughter was enticed to leave school to run the cottage. Local people knitted the Aran sweaters, crocheted the shawls and made the crafts which supplied this small little shop, on wheels, at the gates of Blarney Castle. The first day's trading yielded £14.00 and Christy thought he had struck gold.

Some years later, Christy and his daughter Freda converted the cinema/dancehall into a knitwear factory to supply the cottage with jumpers. This was a small venture, employing ten people.

Meanwhile business at the Mahony's Mills had started to decline and the mill began to feel the squeeze caused by the competition of synthetic materials and world recession. Several attempts were made to bolster the company, but all failed and the mill family wound down production and closed its doors in 1973. The huge stone buildings became bare and empty and the machines were dismantled and removed.

The closing of the mill spelled disaster and had a depressing effect on everyone—not least Christy Kelleher. It saddened him greatly to see the great benefactor fall silent with the resultant job losses impacting greatly on the life of the village.

For two years the great mill lay silent and derelict. Nobody wanted it. Christy visited the site many times and slowly a germ of an idea began to grow—he would buy the buildings he had worked in as a boy and turn the mill into a visitor centre!

There was a family conference and Christy persuaded his wife and children that this was an opportunity not to be missed.

He "did a deal" with the auctioneers and placed a deposit on the Mill only to discover that the financial institutions did not share his enthusiasm.

Christy and Freda met with the banks and had their request for funds refused. What a dilemma! The price was agreed, the deposit was paid and Christy was convinced he was absolutely right.

The family agreed that drastic steps were necessary. The cinema/dancehall had to be sold, homes were re-mortgaged, personal loans taken out by family members and everything really was on the line. Between them, the family raised the funds to purchase the Mill and later persuaded the banks to provide the working capital.

Christy Kelleher was now the proud owner of the woollen mills and one of the first things he did was to remove the iron gate which stood between the Mill and the main road. All the employees of the old Mahony's Mills had only been allowed to enter through a side gate, and Christy was determined that the ordinary people would now be able to go through the main entrance.

The knitwear factory was transferred from the converted dance hall and was the first new activity in the woollen mills. It was a source of great joy to Christy that the Mill was once again being used for manufacturing—it had turned full circle. The old mansion was converted into a hotel—appropriately called Christy's—and the shop transferred into the ground floor of the Mill. The little thatched cottage was taken off the road and today sits proudly in the grounds of Blarney Woollen Mills facing one of the finest visitor reception desks in the country.

The fact that the business prospered is a testament to Christy's dogged enthusiasm and entrepreneurial spirit. He was always there, with a kind word for everyone, welcoming the visitors and encouraging the staff. His unfailing energy and absolute belief in what Blarney could become kept things going through the difficult times.

Nowadays more than a million visitors pass through these old stone buildings each year. The mill has returned to its former position as Blarney's greatest employer with hundreds of people working for The Blarney Group. No visit to Ireland is complete without a stop at the world famous Blarney Woollen Mills.

Christy Kelleher achieved success against all the odds and he was proud of it. He took a fierce pride in his contribution to Blarney

As you can see from the crowded parking lot, the Blarney Woollen Mills is a favorite place of tour companies and visitors alike from all over the world to shop, play, dine, or just rest. This is a place you don't want to miss!

and the economy of Ireland. He instilled in his family a pride in their Irishness and a faith in the future of the nation.

Christy Kelleher, this great man of vision, died in 1991, aged 76. He left behind him a thriving family company, his daughter Freda works in the business daily in her role as Chief Executive, a company that still retains the spirit that made it all possible in the first place. Before he passed away he thanked all of the great people working within these walls for "helping to turn his dream into a reality." He was a man with a dream—but more than that, he was a man with the determination and will to make that dream work—and he did....

Contents above quoted verbatim from materials sent to me by Darren Smyth, executive at Blarney Woollen Mills, in order to preserve the facts accurately.

Contact Information
Darren Smyth
Email: Dsmyth@blarney.com
Website: www.blarneywoollenmills.com
Blarney Woollen Mills Hotel
Blarney County Cork, Ireland
Phone: t353214385011
Fax: t353214385350
Email: info@blkarneywoollenmillshotel.com

Chapter 9

KILLARNEY
The Forgotten

Killarney is located in the South-west of Ireland and has been welcoming visitors for over two hundred years! It has much to see and do, and it is known all over, nationally and internationally, as the center of tourism for this part of the country; in fact, it is said to be the busiest tourist gathering place in rural Ireland. In summer, the traffic on foot, buses, and horses fills the streets. I would rather spend more time in a country town that is not so busy, but it is difficult sometimes to skip where all the other tourists are heading. While you can enjoy the beauty and natural landscape, the commercial scene is alive with enough entertainment and attractions to fit everyone's interests.

The town's attractions include streets lined with more than seventy pubs, and numerous accommodations and restaurants to please any budget and taste. The nightlife is another feature of this town you will not want to miss. We were told by some of the residents that the best time to visit this city is in the off season because the hotels and restaurants raise their prices in the busy season in order to make their profits cover the other months. Now, we can't attest to this as we have only traveled to Ireland in the high season, but I did check rates at other times, and it is a lot less expensive in the off season, but that is true with almost any place you visit.

Killarney's National Park is a nearly twenty-five thousand acre property that was donated to the nation in 1932, and is surrounded by mountains, parklands, and waterways. A highlight of the park and the Muckross House Estate and Gardens is that you can take a jaunting car ride to preserve your energy since visiting there can be a huge walk! A jaunting car is a horse and cart.

Muckross House, a nineteenth century manor and a popular attraction, is situated on the shores of Muckross Lake. The house has two main themes: the environment of the National Park, and nineteenth and twentieth century County Kerry folklore. The gardens are so grand, yet informal, and filled with blooming azaleas and rhododendrons from May through July. There are extensive water gardens and an outstanding rock garden of natural limestone which is a marvel. For those of you who have admired the Butchard Gardens in Victoria, British Columbia, you will also fall in love with these meticulous grounds and wish you could take their gardener home! These grounds are full of history and culture and provide relaxation for the visitor looking to escape the busy hustle of commercial business in Killarney only a five minute drive away. We enjoyed the jaunting ride through this park, stopping to take photos of the deer and wildlife you can see among the trees.

Killarney has fabulous views of the three Lakes of Killarney, and tours are available for either a short water bus (boat) of the largest lake or a longer journey of the three lakes.

The Lakes of Killarney are surrounded by beautiful sandy beaches, high cliffs, and rocky terrain. Many myths surround the famous Lakes of Killarney, from the one about a young woman who, while distracted by her lover, forgot to replace the capstone on her parents' well, thus spilling it out to create the Lakes of Killarney, to the one about a beautiful woman on a white horse who rose from the water and declared it to be the water of eternal youth! While you may not believe these or other myths surrounding these incredible lakes, the folklore and mystery add a pleasant ambiance as you journey about the lakes.

Now, I am a hopeless romantic so I had my own ideas of Killarney, where we had booked a room at Loch Lein Country House Manor, which has a breathtaking view of the lake. I imagined us spending reflective moments on the banks of the water, repeating our marriage vows from twenty-three years earlier (and the twenty-fifth anniversary of our meeting). Of course, I dreamed of a white sundress, flowers in my hair, and a new wedding band with a Celtic design, that includes the Claddagh, since my wedding band was in need of replacement. The story about the Claddagh ring is one of promise, hope of eternal love, and friendship. Please read on and I'll tell you shortly how the details of that romantic idea turned out, and later in Chapter 14, I'll tell you the history of the Claddagh ring.

The many sites of Killarney and surrounding areas will keep you wanting to return again and again, so you too can soak up the magic of this beautiful land.

We made our reservations with the Scott Hotel, which is a beautiful location, but I want to warn you to make sure they don't forget you! We took the combination tours, which meant checking in at the Scotts Hotel Lobby to be picked up and taken to the Park for our jaunting car ride and later to the Ross Castle where we caught the boat that sails the Killarney Lakes. In our case, the Scotts Hotel had assured us it would have someone there to pick us up after the Lake Tour, but it neglected to do so! This was especially important as we were out of the city limits where no taxis or any transportation is available, and to make it worse, there is a steep hill to climb to get to the highway!

I walk with the aid of a cane and we were really stressed. Luckily for us, a tour bus driver took pity on us (again, a friendly Irishman) and gave us a ride to the top of the hill where we then had to walk to the town center.

I am extremely angry that Scotts Hotel did this to us, and I hope you never have this experience. Nor did I receive any apologies or excuses later from them, even after I wrote to them about our disappointment of being abandoned outside of town!

Ross Castle

It also seems, while we paid for a tour, there was more to Ross Castle than what we saw. It was not until we arrived home and I was writing that I discovered the properties surrounding Ross Castle. There are many stories that make this castle tour interesting indeed.

According to what I read, Ross Castle is mostly furnished in the style of the sixteenth and seventeenth centuries which we did not see at all! What we saw were just the ruins of a tower—no one told us there was more. What a shame. Stories have it that the castle is haunted by a lovesick bride named Sabrina whose lover had drowned in Lake Sheelin while en route to whisk her off and elope with her! Being a romantic at heart, I am very sad to have missed this! So again, be sure you get what you pay for, as clearly, we did not.

This tour was not one we would do again, and that has nothing to do with what happened. It was relaxing and the Ross Castle was fine enough to see with the Lakes being very beautiful, but for your money, you can do better. All you really see is a large lake and gorgeous scenery with trees, but you can

see that from the shore. I recommend you skip both trips and just visit the Muckross House and Gardens instead for the best bargain since they are beautiful and speak to you of history.

Chapter 10

LOCH LEIN COUNTRY HOUSE HOTEL
A Slice of Heaven

The Loch Lein Country House Hotel is the most amazing hotel in all of southwestern Ireland. We were pampered beyond belief and so were all the guests! When we asked the owners, Paul and Annette, whether they've ever had any special guests, their reply was quick: "All our guests are equally special." They were amazing hosts in every aspect of our visit. When we drove in to the well-manicured property, they greeted us and offered to help unpack our auto. Then we were checked in as though we were family on vacation coming for a visit! They even escorted us to our room!

Dinner that night was fabulous with three superb entries. Every need or desire was met at this grand location. Wait until you see your rooms. If the words "el-

Top: Loch Lein Country House Hotel—Fossa
Center: Reflecting after Dinner!
Bottom: View from our room

egant, magnificent, comfortable, and million dollar views" come to mind, you probably missed a few positive strokes! Our meals were supervised by Paul, and his wife Annette makes sure you want for absolutely nothing. When you visit, say hello to them for us.

Loch Lein opened its door in 2002, with accommodations for 40-45 guests. You will find there either single or double rooms with a peaceful ambiance that will make your heart flutter with excitement. The feeling that you are about to be pampered beyond your wildest imagination is palpable. Paul and Annette embrace you as though you were long lost family and see to it that all your heart's desires are met, if humanly possible.

In fact, I do not believe they even know the words "No" or "I can't!"

Our Hosts Paul and Annette with us—
Doug and Rosemary

Be sure you take the package here because you do not want to miss out on the cuisine. Both breakfast and dinner are out of this world. Mind you, by the time you get to Fossa (Killarney), you have a good idea of what to expect for meals. But here they go way beyond expectations.

This country house and hotel is a four star property, but once you have stayed there, you will wonder why it isn't a five star rating. It is located on the outskirts of Killarney in a small area known as Fossa and is secluded. It faces the town's lower lake and the Macgillicuddy Reeks, offering the most outstanding views. The Loch Lein Country House Hotel is ideal as a base location to explore the many attractions in the nearby areas, while retiring back to quiet solitude where you can collect your thoughts and make plans for the following day.

Whether you are exploring and shopping in the charming Killarney area, visiting the sites at the famous Ring of Kerry and its stunning scenery, or just staying around to relax by the lakeside, Paul and Annette will help you plan activities and give you the best routes to take.

The twenty-five spacious, double rooms are decorated with simple charm, offering a relaxing space and the assurance you will have everything you need to be fresh and ready to start another adventurous day in the morning. These rooms come complete with all the amenities including a bathrobe in most rooms!

The Legends Restaurant is a peaceful place to find the perfect dining experience after a day of sightseeing or a long drive. You can come back to a tranquil setting and order a drink as you sit by the picture window, restfully looking out at the lake. If you are lucky, maybe you will catch a sighting of the red fox that visits this country hotel. All this is available in the lounge while you rest in cushioned chairs! And this is available to you at most any time of the day! This property is like a Bed and Breakfast with sophistication and style.

Celebrating a wedding, birthday, or anniversary? No problem. Just inform Paul or Annette you want something special and it will happen. Just that easy!

With experienced service and a unique setting, Loch Lein Country House Hotel is an exceptional choice to celebrate your wedding or other special day.

Choose the winding staircase or the elevator

As a matter of fact, we want to share with you a tradition of Ireland we experienced for our own anniversary while at Loch Lein.

Loch Lein is many things for so many people, but after I had discovered the hotel in my research prior to traveling to Ireland, it became clear it was going to be a place for love to bloom—a special place where an anniversary celebration could be alive with spirit and full of excitement. I had an idea that could really make this dream vacation of ours become a romantic episode for the two of us—after all what better for our anniversary than to celebrate it while taking the trip of a lifetime? So let's see if I can take you with me on this journey.

It was an important anniversary for us this year, and we had so much to celebrate. With its lovely presentation, Loch Lein appeared to be exactly what I had been looking for. The descriptions I found in many travel books made it sound as though it would be a wonderful setting for renewing our vows. The day we arrived was such a lovely day that you could smell the breeze as it swept across the lake. In my heart, when I saw the well-kept grounds, I felt like I was in a magazine photo shoot. My surroundings tickled my spirit and filled me with love. That evening, after dinner, Doug and I decided we would take a stroll under the moonlight along the waterside.

(We tried to be quiet so no one would be the wiser and I believe that was accomplished since everyone was so busy that night and I had been ill before our walk, so I am sure the other guests thought we had gone to bed!)

It felt so nice to have the fresh air kiss my face as the breeze brushed against my skirt, reminding me how, many years ago, I had so wanted to recite our wedding vows in this same silly way. I had wanted to be barefoot in a casual white sundress, walking along the sandy beach and saying our vows before God, family, friends, and Nature. And here we were twenty-five years after we first met, still in love, wanting to pledge our love again and forever.

(Now, barefoot would have been a bit much since it was cold and at night so you really wanted to see where your feet were!)

Oh, how it felt to be so in love and celebrate a love that had been strong for so long. We had bought the Claddagh wedding band and were ready for another twenty-five years together. As we professed our love to each other, alone, before the heavens, with wildlife around us, we knew that love had taken us on a journey before and would again for an eternity.

Thank you, Paul and Annette, for having set the mood for us to start a new journey.

RING OF KERRY

A Missed Adventure

Although we missed the drive around the Ring of Kerry, I wanted to share the information so you can decide for yourself whether you want to spend the day driving there. Certainly, most people coming this distance on vacation try to be sure this is part of their activities. However, we were only in the area for one night on our way to Dingle. Perhaps we should have planned better, but by all accounts, The Ring of Kerry was going to be crowded and the highway congested. We wanted to visit places that weren't overrun with tour buses and large crowds so we could meet the locals.

This drive requires at least four hours. If you Google or Bing "The Ring of Kerry," you will see this is Ireland's most popular scenic drive. The Ring of Kerry is actually the name of a small highway that skirts the edges of the Iveragh Peninsula, offering views of pristine lakes, high mountainsides, and a rugged coastline.

While I told you earlier you may want to spend time in Killarney seeing the many shops, they are overrun by tourists and have high prices. All of Killarney is very commercial. So if you want to be part of the real Ireland, you should step out and travel to the smaller towns where people are less likely to be in a rush and are very friendly.

This route along the Ring of Kerry offers the opportunity to visit many such small towns and villages, where food, beverages, and lodging can be found. I believe on a return trip we will take our chances and not make reservations, just take off, planning at least two to three days to do the entire drive. There is a multitude of lodging in Ireland, and I can't help but believe, with as much research as I have done, that one would have no difficulty finding lodging in most of Ireland from B&B's to five star hotels.

Now here, too, is a ferry trip for you to the Skellig Islands if you are strong, brave at heart, and an adventurer! It's a mammoth rock with sharp peaks and a real climb—once inhabited by monks who built beehives out of rock where they could live and pray in severe isolation from the mainland. The ferries do not sail there if the weather is bad, and if you have ever taken a ferry ride on the Atlantic Ocean, believe me, you do not want to be on a boat in bad weather in Ireland! This ferry ride is about a forty-five minute trip and the cost is approximately €40 per person, which is about $60. I would rather see other locations than take a ride almost guaranteed to make me seasick, but it has also been said that to see Ireland, you must travel to the Skelligs! You decide, but research it first.

If you want to find hand knits and linens along the way, it is also reported that Kenmare is a great place to stop for just about anything. And Kenmare is a restful location to spend the night, with a range of accommodations including B&Bs from the very expensive to the nice and inexpensive.

Have a safe journey!

Chapter 11

....

DINGLE PENINSULA

....

Dingle was developed as a port after the Norman invasion. In the thirteenth century, more goods were being exported out of Dingle than Limerick. By the fourteenth century, wine was a major export. During the sixteenth century, Dingle was the major shipping port, exporting fish and hides and importing wines. There is a small river that flows through Dingle Harbor and fishing has always been a part of Dingle's culture. In ancient times, Stone Age men fished the bay.

The Dingle Peninsula will most likely become a topic of conversation with any of you who are thinking of visiting Ireland. It is magical, or at least, many say so! The Dingle Peninsula has been endorsed by National Geographic, Trip Advisor, and CNN. Trip

Top: Waterfront Pier in Dingle
Center: Dingle—as we arrived.
Bottom: Rolling green hills of the Dingle Peninsula

Advisor endorses it as the place to be on New Year's Eve; *National Geographic* described The Dingle Peninsula as "Where Earth and the Heavens Meet!" and CNN said it was "The Most Beautiful Place On Earth." Now that is admiration! Who should know better than them? With endorsements like these, how anyone could not want to go there is a real question.

In Dingle, you can hear traditional Irish music constantly, especially in the evenings and during the summer tourist season. Dingle offers many craft shops, pubs, and restaurants to make your visit there a real experience.

The Dingle Peninsula stretches thirty miles into the Atlantic Ocean along the Southwest coastline of Ireland. The second highest peak in Ireland is Mount Brandon, which stretches into the Slieve Mish mountain range. This beautiful mountain range is the backdrop for the Dingle Peninsula.

The coastline is steep sea cliffs with deep sand splits and the Blasket Islands are just west of the Peninsula. What amazes me is that surfing is very popular here, but the Atlantic is so cold!

The Dingle Peninsula offers many things for residents as well as the tourist. You can find craft stores with hand knit Aran sweaters and fine Irish Linens. If you are not a shopper and want to walk, you will find trails for all ability levels, or you could always walk along the sandy beaches. Entertainment is also available here from traditional dance performances to art and film festivals. Like to ride? Horseback riding is also available. And for those who want to take the day off, you will find some very nice golf courses in the area as well.

If you and your travel partner(s) like to fish, that is available with and without charter services. There is even a safe place for children and adults alike to swim.

Finally, Dingle is an excellent location from which to base yourself while visiting several other areas and sites, such as Killarney, the Ring of Kerry, and the Blasket Islands.

Now, we want to share our Dingle location of residence with you!

THE CAPTAIN'S HOUSE

DINGLE-IRELAND

The Captain's House is located in the center of Dingle town where Jim and Mary began taking in boarders in 1986 and quickly became known for their hospitality and grand meals.

Meet Jim and Mary Milhench

Jim and Mary bought the Captain's House in the 1980s, and with Jim's background, the two of them were able to build a lovely reputation for welcoming guests to their home.

Most every travel or tourist book tells you about the Captain's House and for good reason. But they tell you only the basics, like how Mary cooks up a great breakfast. The fact is, Mary did not cook while we were there due to her husband recovering from surgery and her having recently given birth to twins. By the way—when you stay there be sure to meet those adorable twins! But I will tell you one thing, the kitchen in this unit is laid out like nothing we had ever seen before.

The refrigerator had at least a gallon of milk and a dozen or so eggs, several types of juice, cereals, both hot and cold, fruits, yogurts, a dozen homemade scones, nuts, and the list keeps on going. I would say that you certainly felt welcomed.

Jim and Mary Milhench were two of the nicest people you could ever want to meet, and they certainly know how to run a successful B&B. We have stayed in others we were not sure we would want to try again, but Jim and Mary have changed our minds about B&Bs. Their rates included breakfast and the spread was probably nicer than any buffet anyone would have made for us. The large assortment of food was well thought-out and their generosity was overwhelming. We hope to return for a longer visit!

We arrived in Dingle in the mid-afternoon and when we went looking for the Captain's House we were a bit lost. We had found the front door, but not the entrance to our area. But finally we did and I must admit, when we first approached where we were to enter, I was afraid of what I had gotten us into! The entrance was in an alley and we were worried about our rental car or who might drive through the alley. Keep in mind, if you live in an area at home with alleys that make you nervous, you are not at home so that is not the case here. No worries—we were met at the door and there was absolutely nothing to fear. We entered and had to climb some stairs to our apartment, but once in the apartment, it was one level. As we entered, there was a small dining table with a bowl of fresh fruit and a closet for jackets. To the left was a sofa with coffee table and sitting room complete with television. Further in was the kitchen fully equipped with everything you could even think about needing.

Just beyond the kitchen was our bedroom with a king-sized bed, dark wood dressers, a television, a telephone, and another twin bed. (The king-sized bed was so comfortable. We were extremely relieved since sleeping in strange beds can be difficult, and I do believe the beds here must have had an orthopedic mattress because it felt so NICE!)

The furnishings in the bedroom were done in warm tones and the fine furniture set the mood as we retired. It was very restful. There were hardwood floors that shone with area rugs to warm the feet. The bathroom looked as though it had just been remodeled. It had tiled walls and a large tub/shower area, also done in light warm tones. This is a modest setting and makes you feel as though you are home, and if you desire, you can even do your laundry before leaving!

We will definitely return to Dingle and the Captain's House, which is a great alternative to staying in a hotel room where everything is professionally decorated, as this one appears to be, but you will never feel as much at home as you will here! Thank you, Jim and Mary. Below is the contact information so you can visit the Captain's House. Oh, and when you do, don't forget to take a biscuit for their sweet dog!

Contact Information:
Jim and Mary Milhench
The Mall, Dingle, Co. Kerry, Ireland
Email: captigh@eircom.net
Phone: +353-66-91-51531
Fax: +353-66-91-51079
Months of   April through November
Operation:

Shortly after we checked in, we asked Jim and Mary where we could find a linen store since we were trying to find a bed runner. We had had them in each hotel where we stayed, and I loved the way they dressed up our beds, so I wanted to buy one for home. The one at the Captain's House was about twenty-four inches wide or so, and it ran from side to side, dressing up the end of the bed!

Jim and Mary directed us to the main street where we spent several hours just walking around. They also told us where we could find three pubs on the waterfront side of the city with live traditional music, which I really wanted to hear. It was raining in the late afternoon so we decided to step inside one of the pubs and have lunch, which we thoroughly enjoyed. We had found that most pubs served meals, and they offered the best price as a rule. Some were as good as the fancier restaurants!

Here is a list of the three pubs we were in that day:

John Benny Moriarity's Pub

is located opposite the pier in Dingle and is a great place to eat, drink, and be entertained. Your musical enjoyment is led by John and Eilis who are well known for traditional Irish music and their pub is known as one of the Peninsula's best locations for its attributes. The pub is also known for its food selection, especially the seafood.

This photo of the Traditional Irish Music Duo was taken inside the pub just before the crowd arrived. Then it became standing room only.

Murphy's Pub: Murphy's and John Benny's Pubs are delightful to say the least. We were so happy to find a warm, dry location to wait out the rain. We ended up staying all afternoon and into the night when the Irish band began to play. We had a snack at one location and a fabulous fish and chip dinner in the other. It was difficult to decide which to spend the most time in, as they were both happy places and much fun. Both pubs came highly recommended by Jim and Mary at the Captain's House.

Contact Information:

John Benny Moriarty's Pub
Strand Street, Dingle
Email: johnbennyspub@gmail.com
Website: www.johnbennyspub.com

Murphy's Pub
Strand Street, Dingle
Email: murphyjn@iol.ie
Website: www.murphyspub.ie

Foxy John's Pub: Now, at the risk of making someone angry, I have to tell you we visited Foxy John's Pub and did so because many travel books talk about it being the place to be. We found it to be a place where you walk in and leave as quickly as possible. It claims to be both a pub and a hardware store, but well, as far as a hardware store goes, let's just say it was not stocked for business. And it certainly was no pub we wanted to stay in since it was not particularly clean. Perhaps it was supposed to be a draw for its wild idea of having a hardware store inside a pub! At any rate, we found ourselves enjoying the other two pubs where food, music, friendly people, and atmosphere all existed.

In closing, The Dingle Peninsula offers the tourist so much, and if you can allow yourself the time to explore it, you'll find the real town of Dingle and not just the commercial side. You will see where it appears that the land reaches up to the heavens and the sea flows into the very core of town, all surrounded by the wonder of majestic mountains. It is a place where the sand beneath your feet makes you feel as though you have reached the perfect place to stay and it makes you yearn to return.

On the Dingle Peninsula, we noticed that the local population had a heavier tongue and the sounds of their voices still ring a tone of delight in my ears and memories. It is also a place where the small town reaches out with every possible welcoming attitude. You will find a place where talents seem to be endless as you observe the local crafts displayed in the stores: Aran sweaters, bedding, pottery woodcarvings, and so much more. We found all these things and more.

Remember to visit the local pubs, but be aware that some pubs are a better choice than others. The waterfront areas have really entertaining pubs, and there are also some on the main and side streets as well.

Want to surf the Net while in Dingle? There is a waterfront cafe where you can do just that! Yes, we found it ourselves, and they had many computers to use, but what we wanted was a charger for my iPad, so we could have it charging while traveling, and so I could continue to write about our trip. It was a great find here in this café.

Dingle's Famous Dolphin

FUNGI

Fungi is a playful Bottlenose Dolphin that took up residence in Dingle in 1984. It is estimated that he was born in the mid-1970s, which makes him really old now. Some say he is not wild but was somehow released from an aquarium. Others say he just likes it in Dingle and would rather spend time with humans than his own species.

During summer, Fungi has been observed catching Garfish at the mouth of the harbor. Garfish are not normally dolphin fare. In the winter, Fungi travels further out to catch his meals. It seems that Fungi has found his home in Dingle and his job! He escorts the fishing boats to and from port, assigning himself as the pilot! It apparently only took him nine months to develop from a shy, curious dolphin to a dolphin that loved to play with human visitors and be their companion! Fungi has been known to interact with swimmers, boaters, divers, and children.

There is a bronze sculpture of Fungi in Dingle. He is a major tourist attraction, with businesses capitalizing on his fame. Fungi souvenirs from postcards to stuffed animals are found in almost any store catering to the tourist trade. Fear has it that if Fungi should pass, the town will suffer economic loss, and with the average age of his species being twenty-five, it could happen at any time. Fungi has become like a family member, or at the least a cherished friend, to countless people all over the world. His passing will certainly be a sad day. This is one commercial tourist activity that will bring you pleasure, so if you have the time, enjoy visiting with Fungi, and be sure to take your camera!

Dingle Town, thank you! We will be back!

Chapter 12

DOOLIN
A Busy Port

Doolin is a pretty little town with an assortment of hotels, B&Bs, hostels, restaurants, pubs, souvenir shops, a golf course, a cave, and a Castle Hotel. There many things to see and do here, but the ferries that take you to the Aran Islands are Doolin's main attraction.

Doolin—another Piece of Heaven!

Doolin is a small village found on the Northwest coast of County Clare in the Shannon region along the Atlantic coast. This small village seems to be known worldwide and is associated with being the Irish Traditional Music capitol of Ireland, according to various sources.

Dating back to the 1970s, when popular Irish whistle players lived in Doolin, this little town began to attract tourists to hear the sounds of Irish folk music and Doolin quickly became famous.

The main street (for all intents and purposes, the only street) is Fisher where most of the activity takes place and where most of the businesses, lodging, stores, and pubs are found. But then, of course, you will find community if you venture up any of the small roads. Oh, and by the way, be sure to have cash on hand because there do not seem to be any ATMs in town! There are limited lodgings, so make reservations if you plan on staying in town.

Doolin is one of only three locations that have a ferry service to the Aran Islands. If you make ferry reservations prior to arrival, I suggest you ask for a refund guarantee. The ferries don't sail in bad weather and refunds are not mandatory. You should also be aware that there are several boat lines that depart from Doolin, so shop around for the best boat and not just the best buy!

Believe me, this is not where you want to economize. Look for the largest boat for this trip, or better yet, read on to see why you should find an alternative way to see the Aran Islands.

You can also find numerous archeological sites dating back to the Iron Age, which could prove to be of real interest.

Rock climbing and surfing are big sports in Doolin, attracting tourists and locals alike. Still want more to see? Doolin is a great jumping off point for a trip to the Cliffs of Moher. These cliffs are another must see.

We are sad to say our visit to Doolin was brief and we left unhappy about our trip to the Aran Islands and the Ballinalacken Castle Hotel. Read on to find out why and how you can avoid making the same mistakes.

We know now what we should have done, and we will plan the next trip accordingly since we want to return here—this little town is truly a piece of heaven!

Just Plain Ole Facts!

1. The River Aille runs from the Hills of the Burren right past Doolin to the Sea.
2. Crab Island is mostly barren, except for some remains of the nineteenth century stone constabulary outpost. It is also a hangout for surfers!
3. Ferry services are available from Doolin to the Cliffs of Moher.
4. Doolin is divided into four parts according to sources found on the Internet:

   Harbor: Departing ferries to the Aran Islands and Cliffs of Moher

   Fisher Street: Pub and businesses

Roadford: Many B&Bs, two hostels, two pubs, and four restaurants

Fitz's Cross: two new hotels, hostel, pub, campsite

5. Population: Approximately 500

6. Doolin Cave: longest stalactite discovered in the Northern hemisphere

Our first glimpse at Doolin

7. Doolin is known for its surfing and rock climbing
8. Two of the four pubs were founded in the 1800s
9. Best location to Stay for Value, Quality and Location: Doolin Hotel
10. Gus O'Connor's Pub—sources say it is the greatest Pub in Ireland offering Traditional Music as well! Now, considering there are thousands of pubs or so it seemed, that is saying a lot!
11. Shannon Airport: reported as 40 miles from Doolin
12. Distance to: Galway 45 miles; Dublin 160 miles

ARAN ISLAND FERRIES

"The Trip from Hell"

It was rainy and overcast the day we took our tour to the Aran Islands from Doolin. We were to go to Inis Mor, but the people at ARAN2 Ferries said the waters to that location were too rough. Instead they had us get on the ferry to Inis Oirr.

We were on a schedule and did not really want to go to Inis Oirr. We had planned to take the ferry to the Cliffs of Moher and Inis Mor, where the largest craft stores and sweater factories were reportedly located. We were told to go to Inis Orr, and when we got back, we could talk about taking the trip we had booked and paid for in advance.

I asked what the trip was going to be like to Inis Oirr since the waters were too rough to travel to Inis Mor. They just said it would be fine and to hurry or we would not be going anywhere that day. Their attitude was not very nice, but we went anyway, as did many others.

The ARAN2 people said it would be fine on the water to Inis Oirr and assured us Inis Oirr had lots of sweaters and sweater mills also. Well, that was ALL NOT TRUE!

For beginners, the water was not fine. When we first pushed off, everyone was excited about the motion, putting their arms up in the air, and yelling, "Woooooo!" as though they were on a rollercoaster! Within ten minutes, no one was laughing and almost everyone was having trouble standing up. I told Doug I did not feel too great, and he managed to get up and go tell the crew I needed help.

They came immediately to help me to the back of the boat to get some fresh air, but it was so rough they fell over on top of me! We reached the back and they sat me down along with several others. Shortly, they were busy trying to help almost everyone hold the plastic bags we had been given, as most of us got violently sick.

Those who could not stand the odor, including Doug, went outside on the deck to get some fresh air, only to be drenched from the waist down by waves splashing over the deck.

Have you ever seen *Deadliest Catch* on television? That is how the water was on that day! Or so it seemed to most of us.

When we finally arrived forty-five minutes later, the crew asked me how I was. I told them I did not want to get back on the boat, but they informed me there was no other way to get back to Doolin!

The crew said it would not be as bad on the return trip. BUT IT WAS!

To make things worse, when we arrived at Inis Oirr, our transportation choices were vans, or a horse and trap (a horse drawn cart). Trap seemed like a treat. At least that's what we thought at the time. But I wanted no part of getting on or into anything that moved. I was still sick so walking was a far better option!

Everyone had left the docks except us and a few who were sick. By the time we were ready to move along, the only transportation left was one horse and buggy—and its driver was not about to let us alone! He was an older man and persistent. He followed us around until we decided he may just need the financial help (we did not want to hurt or insult him either). So, we decided we would hire his service after my stomach settled down.

We walked in the fresh air for a while and then ducked into the nearest pub when it started to rain. Doug had a beer as I sipped on a Coke to settle my stomach. While we were relaxing, this gentleman with the Horse and Cart (Trap) came in to see whether we were still interested. He just didn't give up. We had no idea what to pay him, so Doug asked the bartender. The bartender said we should not agree to more than €20 for the two of us.

We talked to the driver and agreed on €20 for a ride around the island. Although persistent, the driver seemed to be a kind and soft spoken older gentleman. While we were riding around, I kept telling him I wanted to stop at the craft store to look for Aran sweaters. He kept telling me his wife made them, too. He had us stop at a home where the people were very nice, but the sweaters there were for small children. Again, I told him to take us to the store where there was supposed to be a large selection. Instead, he stopped at another home. And this one only had one sweater and it was made for a very large man. The driver kept asking whether we wanted to see this or that attraction, and since we didn't know anything about this island that we had never planned to visit, we just said, "Fine" and let him take us where he wanted.

When we finally returned to the dock, he charged us more than twice the agreed upon price! He hadn't taken us to a single sweater mill. Just a few private homes where we were shown a total of three sweaters! It was not a productive or pleasant day. Well, except for the absolutely beautiful surroundings.

When it was time to go back, a tour group showed up, edged their way ahead of everyone else, and took most of the seats. When we did get on, Doug had to ask someone to move their books so I could sit down. (I sure did not want to be on a boat at that point.) As we were boarding, I had asked again how the water was going to be and was told it would not be bad at all, which was also inaccurate. Doug had to stand all the way back and this time we were both sick!

Do yourself a favor. Go to Galway and fly to Inis Mor. It only takes ten minutes or so, not the advertised forty-five, or the actual hour and twenty minutes by boat. And you will not be seasick when you get there!

If you insist on going by boat, talk to all the ferry lines. There are several to choose from. ARAN2 was not compassionate; nor did it refund our money, even though it took us to the wrong island! And later, they would not discuss the make good trip they had mentioned when they were rushing us onto the boat to Inis Oirr.

This was a good lesson for us since we had been so trusting about everything on this trip, but now we had our eyes wide open!

Lesson learned: Buyer Beware!

All in all, we had only three issues in Ireland in three weeks, and two of them happened on this trip to Inis Oirr. Please do not let these minor issues keep you from enjoying Inis Oirr or Ireland, should you choose to visit.

Sorry, I was too sick to take photos on the boat ride.

Please enjoy the many photos of our time on the Island itself. Although it was a disappointment, it was a lovely location to visit. We have many photos to share with you. The island (as told to us) has had its share of financial difficulties and perhaps that is why things happened as they did. In the following story, we will share some of the many sites we saw and some facts about this little island and the people we so enjoyed meeting.

ARAN ISLANDS

Inis Oirr

Inis Oirr, according to my research, is the smallest and most
beautiful of the three Aran Islands (we only saw the one so
we cannot tell you for sure). It
is the closest island to the main-

O'Flatharta Pub-Restaurant and Hotel

land and is completely surrounded by clear, icy-blue waters. My research
indicated the population is around 250 people. However, the numbers we
saw in the pub indicate this number expands in the summer as tourists
flock to the island. Many of these tourists are looking for the famous Aran
sweaters!

Most of the homes we observed were modest, and the way of life seemed to
be laid back with no one in much of a hurry. Each person we passed offered
up a smile and a hello. We were totally amazed at all the rocks everywhere.
The driver told us the rock fences were more a place to put the large number of rocks cleared from the fields than a means to fence off property.

I will say that Inis Oirr has the
most beautiful scenery I have
ever seen in such a small space.
It was obvious to us this community was close knit and had a
strong Celtic influence. Inis Oirr
is located in the middle of Galway Bay and almost appears as
though neither time nor indus-

try has spoiled the natural beauty of this island. Inis Oirr also appears to
be untouched by industrial and technological advances that can change a
special place forever.

Inis Oirr is traditionally self-sufficient with a farming and fishing based
economy. But according to our driver, only large commercial vessels ca-

pable of getting away from the coastline are still viable. The decline in fishing caused financial setbacks and led to economic dependence on the mainland. We were also told that daily supplies had to be delivered from the mainland; that need caused a certain amount of sadness to the residents here because they no longer felt they were as strong a community as they once were.

Many sources say visiting the island in winter is magical, but I have to say the seas were rough enough in June. Imagine what they would be like traveling in winter. I love a storm at the coast, but I want to watch it with my feet on the land. Based on my recent travel—my stomach still gets upset when I see an ocean scene with wild waves—I think I'll pass on the winter excursion!

This is the stretch of water we crossed on our way to Inis Oirr. We took this picture after we were on dry land!

One really positive aspect of this island is its people. Everyone seemed genuinely happy to see the tourists arrive. The sincerity in their hearts reflected in their eyes and made us feel so welcome.

Although the boat was really crowded and the pub busy, we did not see many people on the streets, or anyone just roaming around town. It was quiet and peaceful, and if we had not known differently, we would have concluded the townspeople were either away, in the pub, or they had simply deserted the island. That is how still this small island appeared to us. Inis Oirr had the mentality of a small bright town with the ability to shut out the world around it. How nice it would be to escape the worries of a big city life! I am not sure you or I could ever relax on the beaches of Inis Oirr, but only because it is not warm. The beaches are inviting and make you want to take off your shoes and walk on the sand, but it is too cold. If you did decide to do so, it would be in complete privacy since the beach is deserted with the exception of the occasional bird flying overhead. Because my stomach was in no mood to eat, we missed out on what I kept hearing was a delight here—fresh crabs, my favorite!

I have not researched the third Aran Island, Inis Meain, but it is most likely charming and worth a visit. If I may make a recommendation, try to visit all of the Aran Islands, if it is at all possible.

Check out the flight from Galway. Perhaps you will be able to find some type of special that includes all three islands. You can fly with Aer Arann out of Galway for a modest price, or ferry

Top: Doug in the O'Flatharta Pub at Inis Oirr
Bottom: Town of Inis Oirr

across from Doolin in the summer or from Inverin all year round. You may want to plan a day and night on the islands so you can enjoy the evening activities as well and get to know the locals in a different way—learning what the real Ireland is like!

BALLINALACKEN CASTLE HOTEL

"Our Worst Two Nights in All of Ireland"

Greetings Fellow Travelers!

Before we start, we would like to tell you this is not written in anger. We know we are running the risk of making some angry, and for that we are sorry, but the truth is important to us. We simply did not get value for our dol-

Ballinalacken Castle Hotel

lar, so we wanted to tell you what we endured in hopes you will not make the same mistake we did.

I read all the reviews written before we were guests at the Ballinalacken Castle Hotel and they were mostly positive, so I have to wonder why it was the way it was for us. Was it solely because the owners did not like booking agencies as they told us? Are there good rooms for direct reservations and not so good rooms for the booking agency reservations? If that is so, and after reading the reviews, you still want to visit this site, be sure to book your room directly with the Castle Hotel. Be sure you ask for the room pictured on the website if that is what you want.

REMEMBER, this is a castle hotel, not a refurbished castle. The actual castle, while interesting, is in ruins. Here you must be specific and request that your requirements come back to you in writing! The people who run this place are very nice, but that is not enough!

These two nights spent in Doolin were the worst two nights of our Ireland trip and we were in the country for almost three weeks (twenty days). We were so excited to have been booked in a castle for part of our anniversary celebration! My mistake. It was a castle hotel. Okay, we could live with that, but not the rest of it.

As we approached this difficult to locate hotel, we looked at one another and wondered what kind of five star hotel would look like what we were seeing! They were obviously in the midst of working on things since they were painting the hotel in this awful, dead mustard color and the place was in much need of TLC!

The interior was much more pleasing. The lobby was decorated with antiques as was the library and dining area. The hotel is not a handicapped friendly establishment, so it will not work for you if you cannot climb stairs.

The owner's daughter-in-law, Cecilia, was pleasant enough, but she let us know within the first fifteen minutes that she did not like Booking.Com or other reservation agencies. I thought that was odd, since Cecilia had said no one would know about this location or its availability without reservation agencies.

Cecilia politely showed us to our room. When we got there, I asked her what had happened to our four poster bedroom with a separate sitting room looking out to the sea. She said it was given to someone else. (REMEMBER, I told you SHE DID NOT LIKE reservations from booking agencies and she did not put anyone from the booking agencies in those rooms.)

I told her I had been writing to her for some time with no response, instructing that it was our holiday in Ireland and we were looking to book the room I described above. She said they had not received any of the MANY emails I had sent, except the last two.

We were upset to say the least. Both Cecilia and the clerk told us our room had been changed because the hotel was sold-out and someone had given the room to another guest just the night before, right out from under us again! WOW!

The room we expected and requested is, by the way, the photo the hotel shows on its website. Cecilia walked us down the hall so we could see that room and it was exactly the room we had expected. She promised to move us to it the next night as the occupants were only staying one night.

The next morning, as we were leaving to spend the day on the Aran Islands, Cecilia said not to worry; she would have our belongings moved not to the actual room but to one exactly like it. She said she had noticed I walk with a cane so the alternate room was more accessible, but it would be exactly like the one on the website and the one she had shown us in terms of its type of bed, style, and spaciousness!

Were we surprised with our new room on our return! The scenario had just become worse and

Very tired as we depart for the Aran Islands

worse. There was a four poster bed and a table with a view and two chairs, but wait until you see the pictures.

When you first see the bed, you immediately see the lumps in the mattress. Just to be fair, I looked up under the sheets. By the way, the sheets had just been laid on the bed, not tucked. The blankets were pulled halfway up on the bed. The sheets and blankets were not bunched up, so we knew it was the mattress.

We had two large suitcases and two smaller ones and we were unable to lay them out or even stow them anywhere, since there was no space to walk around. The bed and table with two chairs took up all the space and you had to walk sideways to move in the room. When I went to wash my hands in the bathroom, the faucet just twisted around on the sink—no hot water either! The curtains were falling down off a few hooks and there were cracks in the walls.

Guess what? We wanted to check out. We didn't want to pay for another night in this dump, which was nothing like what we were sold. Their policy, as we had learned, was no refunds for early check outs, but there was no way we were staying. I would just contest the charges when we got home. (They did end up issuing a refund for the one night we left early, but nothing for the miserable misrepresented rooms.)

After I called the desk about leaving early, I heard a knock at the door. It was the hotel clerk who wanted to show me another room so we would not depart sooner than we had planned to stay. Their policy in the high season was a reservation for three nights, but after dealing with it one night and then receiving worse accommodations the next, we were not going to stay the third. Two nights were all we could handle! The clerk actually showed me three other rooms, but not one was the room we were promised. I asked her, "How is it that you have rooms to show me when you said you were sold-out earlier?" Her reply was that they would just give someone else our room! There was no way we were going to do that to someone else, so we stayed in the unpleasant room and checked out in the morning, after two nights. What a disappointment as we were truly sad that after traveling all this distance, we had no memories to share about a special stay in a castle.

After arriving back home, I reviewed our photos of the room they moved us to and it was exactly as I remembered—awful!

Our advice to you is, do not believe photos on websites. Ask questions, and somehow be sure you will get what you pay for. This hellish site cost us WAY upwards of $150 a night. They had also advertised free Internet, but it was only in the bar and had a weak signal. No Internet service was available in the rooms.

The only positive thing we can say about this place was the meal we enjoyed our first night was simply delightful. The breakfast was also worth bragging about. The food was simply a beautiful presentation, generous and delightful. This property really shines for its meals. If you are in Doolin, we do not recommend you stay here, but we definitely do suggest you stop in to enjoy the pleasure of a meal.

The second night we went to a wonderful restaurant called Sheedy's Hotel and Restaurant in Lisdoonvarna, which was only a short drive away. This is a beautiful location and simply amazing. I wish we had stayed there, but the hotel was sold-out!

When we made our reservations, we read almost all of the reviews written about Ballinalacken Castle Hotel, but found only a few negatives. There are always a few negative reviews, so we felt the majority would be correct. But now our advice to you is: Do not stay there. But also remember, this experience is not the same one you will find in other castle hotels.

Check the locations you book in several sources and read as much as you can before deciding. In fact, other than making sure there are rooms available in a few very special places, you could do the whole trip without making any reservations.

Once when we were a bit lost, we found a five star hotel: The Ashford Castle. The Ashford was not like the Ballinalacken Castle Hotel in any fashion. And it is actually a Castle! I know of a woman who stayed there for two weeks with her mother. It was the only place they made reservations and they had no trouble whatsoever there, or finding other places to stay when they visited whatever B&B or hotel they came upon while traveling.

The Ballinalacken Castle Hotel was to be our one castle stay in Ireland and we were so disappointed!

Making New Canadian Friends

One good thing about our Ballinalacken stay was the new friends we made. Actually, we met John and Heather that blissful day when we first stayed at the Loch Lein Country House Manor and were planning to renew our vows. At suppertime, we were seated in the corner of the dining room where we had a bit of privacy and enjoyed a glass of wine prior to dinner. We were talking to the owner who had walked up to the table when John turned to say a word to Paul (the owner of Loch Lein), and suddenly, we were engaged in a conversation with John and his wife, Heather. The evening progressed and we discovered they were from Canada, had made their

own reservations as we had, and we were all heading to the same area in a few days. And staying in the same location! A coincidence or meant to be? I believe in fate, so I believe we were meant to be friends!

Even stranger events later showed us that our friendship was meant to be. Somehow, although we left at different times and went in different directions, we ended up on the same ferry boat to Doolin. Then we arrived almost the same time at the Castle Hotel. Fate was sealed and that evening was spent with our new friends en-

joying dinner and the pleasures of a stimulating conversation. After dinner, we all took a tour of the real Ballinalacken Castle's ruins.

The most comical part of our stay at Ballinalacken was the crazy donkey that kept trying to eat my coat or my cane! Our wonderful new friends kept trying to protect me!

CLIFFS OF MOHER

A Reality Check on Water Conditions!

The mind races and heartbeats grow faster as you approach these cliffs. When you are near the Cliffs of Moher, you can almost see yourself getting caught up in the crashing waves.

These Giants offer an exciting view that is sure to capture your heart. We viewed them up close and personal from the sea on a boat tour. The majestic site is

Top: The best part of our Castle Hotel stay—our new friends, John and Heather from Canada!
Bottom: The Cliffs of Moher!
What an incredible view!

one we will carry with us forever. Close your eyes and imagine being in a small boat on the Atlantic Ocean and motoring up to the enormous Cliffs of Moher, which are a sheer 600 foot rise from the Atlantic Ocean and stretch for nearly five miles. The cliffs are made of great, dark sandstone. You can't help feeling like a small pea in a large barrel.

The sounds of screaming sea birds hung in the air as the birds wheeled and swooped about the waves. This was real excitement of a kind we have never felt before. The best view, other than from the boat tour, is from O'Brien's Tower. The tower was built in 1853, by Cornelius O'Brien. It can be seen and photographed from the Cliffs of Moher center. There you will climb many stairs to the top where a breathtaking view of these giants awaits.

We believe that, although there are other ways to view these miracles, our small boat tour is the best way to experience the grandeur of these amazing cliffs that are majestic in every way! But be warned again—the waters

are not for the weak at heart or stomach!

The Cliffs are named for Fort Mothar, a promontory fort that no longer exists except for a few ruins. It was destroyed during the Napoleonic wars so a signal tower could be constructed.

The waters are not so calm as they smash against the giant rock formations of the Cliffs of Moher.

The Cliffs are one of Ireland's largest attractions and the cost of visiting them can add up quickly. Parking alone is about $12.00. But if you are handicapped, you can park for free as long as you have the proper parking placket, so be sure you pack yours should you have one. At least it was that way for us at the time. There is also a package price for approximately €6.00 per person ($9.00 U.S.) and children under sixteen are free. This charge includes access to the center, admission to the Cliffs Exhibition, Atlantic Edge, and parking. The balance goes to the conservation and safety of the Cliffs. Other types of offers are available, such as senior and student discounts as of the time of this writing.

Then, of course, there are several souvenir stands, both inside and outside the center building. Inside you will find films of the Cliffs. This set-up made no sense to us since the real view was right out the door and up the steps. The center took over seventeen years to plan and construct, costing more than €32 million. It opened in February 2007 and was built right into a hillside, in an attempt to stay in keeping with the sensitivities of the environment. The center also uses renewable energy systems, like solar panels, and works hard to conserve energy in as many ways as possible.

Other than those unable to make the climb, I can't imagine why anyone would want to watch these wonders on a television screen when the cliffs are so close you feel as though you could touch them. It is too bad they don't offer motorized carts to take the handicapped up to the top. I myself walked with the help of a cane and it took a long while to get to the top, but there was no way, after traveling so far, I was going to miss exploring the grounds or miss the view from the Cliffs themselves.

You can buy everything from t-shirts to crystal here. But if you are really good, it will only cost you the parking charges. Don't plan on that, though. Drinks, snacks, maybe lunch, and shirts will easily add up to at least $20 per person.

The Cliffs of Moher are a major habitat for cliff nesting birds, which is why you will observe so many flying on and off the Cliffs. The birds are protected in this area and for a certain distance over the water to ensure their safety. The majestic awe of this site will touch your heart like nothing else in Ireland. It is Nature at its best! If you do not arrive by boat, you will hear the roar of the sea as it pounds against the Cliffs long before you ever see them.

The Cliffs are made mainly of Namurian shale and sandstone. Many animals, mostly birds, inhabit the cliffs. I believe the Atlantic Puffin is commonly found here so you will find it on most of the souvenirs inside the center, including Puffin shot glasses and sweatshirts! It is said that over 30,000 birds call these cliffs home.

The Cliffs of Moher have been used as a backdrop for many music videos and films, including: *Leap Year* from 2010, *Harry Potter and the Half-Blood Prince* from 2009, and Maroon 5's *Runaway,* to name a few.

The Moher Tower is a stone ruin of the old watchtower that sits on Hag's Head located at the southern end of the Cliffs of Moher. It is a single tower, almost square style. It is in ruins with no inhabitants, except the choughs, which are crow-like birds. Its history is unknown according to sources I found on the Internet, and it is located at the top of the stairs climbing out to the Cliffs view.

This photo gives you some idea of how far it is to the tower from below.

In November 2011, the Cliffs of Moher were one of twenty-eight global finalists for the "New Seven Wonders of Nature." Although they didn't make the final list of seven, no one can deny that they are one of God's natural wonders, without the hands of man to alter them, so be sure not to miss them.

Enjoy your time here and plan to spend at least three to four hours.

Chapter 13

LISDOONVARNA

The unique area of Lisdoonvarna has so much to offer the traveler. You can relax and be pampered at one of the magical spas, shop until you're ready to rest in comfort, visit the beautiful property of Sheedy's, or simply sit and read up on activities you want to try the next day, while sipping a favorite beverage.

Lisdoonvarna is located in the heart of the Burren region and is a popular tourist area. Its name comes from the Gaelic "Lios Dhuin Bharna," meaning lios or enclosure of the fort in the gap. Lisdoonvarna has many interesting places to explore and enjoy, some dating back to the Iron Age and the pre-Christian era, but it is best known for its healing Spa Center.

Lisdoonvarna transports you back to the eighteenth century when a Limerick surgeon discovered that the mineral waters had positive effects on his patients. People were soon coming from all around to "bathe in and drink the mineral waters which were rich in iron, sulphur, magnesium and calcium and were said to provide relief for certain diseases."[1]

When visiting in June, we saw a quiet, peaceful setting. We really enjoyed this small town while we were there.

In researching the town, what we read about the most was the Matchmaking Festival in September. During the festival this small town of 800 people has over 40,000 visitors.

---

1 From http://www.myguideireland.com/lisdoonvarna

Because the Matchmaking Festival is long-standing tradition, we thought we would provide some information for all our single readers looking for a mate!

MATCHMAKING FESTIVAL

The Matchmaking Festival is a tradition that began a couple of hundred years ago, and has been celebrated in Lisdoonvarna for 150 years. Although the festival's name implies its purpose, thousands of people flock to Lisdoonvarna every September in search of a good time, and if they happen to meet up with someone special, then it's a bonus. The festivities begin on September 1 and continue all month, ending the first few days in October. Today, according to the records I read, there is only one official matchmaker left in County Clare, Mr. Willie Daly, who helps people at the festival to make a match.

This festival has become one of Europe's largest singles events. The songs and celebration last into the night with dancing from noon until the wee hours of the next morning. Dance exhibitions and traditional music are also a large part of the activities.

Other Lisdoonvarna Events and Attractions

The Lisdoonvarna Horse Racing Festival, The Marching Band Festival Weekend, and the annual Irish Barbeque Championships all lasting three days are an additional part of the long celebration for the Matchmaking Festival in September.

Lisdoonvarna is also close to such attractions as the Cliffs of Moher, the Burren, the Dingle Peninsula, where the rugged North Atlantic coast is known for its Angling, as well as other popular fishing opportunities. All in all, this area is another grand location where many benefits are waiting just for you.

So, whatever your plans in this town, enjoy the people and sites!

SHEEDY'S COUNTRY HOUSE HOTEL & RESTAURANT

An Unforgettable Experience

This experience is another we simply must tell you, "DO NOT MISS!"

Up to this point in our Ireland journey, we had experienced many different adventures from some grand disappointments to some of the most exciting moments of a lifetime. Sheedy's Country House Hotel and Restaurant definitely belongs in the latter group.

In fact, if you are going to visit Doolin, we suggest you drive a few minutes further and stay and dine at Sheedy's in Lisdoonvarna. It is a convenient location for reaching the Aran Islands or touring the Cliffs of Moher, although we advise you instead to do it the way we described previously.

The owners of Sheedy's, John and Martina, will hold your attention with their charm, wit, and compassion, and you will feel you have become a part of their extended family.

As you approach the entrance of this three-hundred year old family home, you first have to walk past the lovely flower garden and walkway. On an evening with a mild breeze, as was the case when we were there, the aroma from the roses and sweet flowers sets the mood for what you will find once you open the doors to Sheedy's. If first impressions tell you what you can expect, then you will feel extreme satisfaction from the time you drive up until you leave.

Sheedy's was quite different from anywhere we had ever been before. In the past, when we had dined out, we were taken to the dining area and waited to be served.

Not so here! We were led to the foyer next to the fire, where we could sit and enjoy a beverage of our choice and some fabulous hors d'oeuvres. They were our first taste of John's fabulous cooking. Here is a quote taken from Sheedy's website about John's cooking that is certainly true enough!

Meet John

"John started his career as a chef in the mid 1980s in the Michelin Star restaurant of the Plaza Athénée in Paris before returning to Ireland to the Blue Book Property, Longueville House in Mallow Co. Cork.

"While at Longueville, he was responsible for a team that earned the restaurant five Michelin Bib Gourmand ratings over five different years. The bib Gourmand rating means the restaurant is a Michelin inspector's favorite for good food at moderate prices—a principle that John stands over in his own restaurant at Sheedy's in Lisdoonvarna."

John does all the cooking with only one person to help him with the prep work.

John moved on from the Longueville House to the world renowned Ashford Castle as Chef for nine years and afterwards cooked for many dignitaries at the opening of Ellis Island. He even did a program on World Class Cuisine for the Discovery Channel, so you can see what an incredible treat your palettes are in for when you dine at Sheedy's. With all John's experience, you would think Sheedy's would have a "Stuck Up" atmosphere with matching hosts, but it is just the opposite!

Sheedy's Hotel and Restaurant is one of the most immersive and compassionate locations in all of the country. You will not leave here hungry or mistreated.

Martina makes sure each guest is treated as though he or she were her only guest, with several visits to your table during dinner to be sure that your service, meal, and even beverage is all that you expected and more. Martina

is a very pleasant and kind woman with only one thing on her mind—
YOU!

How nice it felt to be pampered like this. We can honestly say, after three
weeks of dining out (and a week we spent in the Caymans before we visited
Ireland), that we experienced only two places that catered to their customers like this, and Sheedy's is one of them!

Martina met John while she
was also in the employ of Ashford Castle. They were married and bought Sheedy's Hotel
from John's parents. They made
Sheedy's a warm, inviting dream
for you to enjoy while you explore this part of Ireland. You
DO NOT want to miss out on

Say hello to Martina

this fabulous location where every wish can come true!

John and Martina have two lovely children, Matthew age eight, and Roisin
age five. Now, it would be my guess that John and Martina have these two
young children learning the restaurant trade in both the kitchen and out
front with the customers. The whole family lives together in a converted
barn next to the Hotel, which is uniquely faced with seventeenth century
stone.

In 1935, Sheedy's began as a farmhouse where John's great-grandmother
took in guests. It has been in the family since its conception. In 1998, John
and Martina bought the property from John's parents after they had spent
many years working various jobs while he perfected his culinary skills.

Sheedy's comes equipped with eleven rooms, six with double-beds (two are
six-foot wide beds), and five rooms with twin beds. Rates range from only
€99 to €180 per room and they are open April through October.

The restaurant has a seating capacity of twenty-five and both breakfast and
dinner are served.

Sheedy's employs five full-time employees and two part-time workers. When I asked Martina to give me just one quote for our readers, she said, "We pride ourselves in being a family run hotel giving traditional hospitality and service."

Be sure to visit their website for more interesting facts and photos at www. sheedys.com.

Please say hello to both John and Martina when you visit. We're sure you will find that Sheedy's is a dream come true!

Enjoy!

Now, I would like to share with you a sample of Sheedy's menu so you can see for yourself that a visit here is a bargain. The full menu contains many additional items not included here.

APPETIZERS

Warm Tart of Local Organic St Tola Goats Cheese
Carpacchio of Beetroot, Caramelised Onions and Figs, Red Wine Syrup
€9.50

Pan Seared Scallops
Served with a Sherry and Red Pepper Sauce
€12.50

Fresh Homemade Soup of the Evening
€6.00

BAR MENU

Salad of Roasted Pear with Cashel Blue Cheese Dressing
€5.50

Smoked Salmon Platter served with Homemade Brown Bread
Starter Size €9.00 Main Course Size €16.00

Slow Cooked Beef, served with Horseradish Mash and Red Wine Sauce
€17.00

Main Course Size Crab Claws in Garlic Butter
€22.50

Fresh Fish in Homemade Beer Batter with Mushy Peas and Tartar Sauce
€18.50

Freshly Made Omelette
of Local Organic Eggs and Smoked Salmon served with Side Salad
€11.50

MAIN COURSE DISHES

Lamb
Roast Rack of Burren Lamb with Mustard and Parsley Crust, Spinach and Confit of Shoulder, Lamb Jus
€28.00

Sirloin Steak
Prime Irish Hereford Steak Served with Braised Shallots, Horseradish & Chive Mash and Red Wine Sauce
€28.00

Fresh Fish of the Day
Baked Fillets of Fish served with a Mild Spanish Red Pepper Sauce
€28.00

Pork Belly
Slow Cooked Caramelised Belly of Pork with Mustard Mash, Madeira Sauce
€24.50

Our lamb is sourced from Bernard Roughan, Ennistymon

We always use Irish Beef

Our fish is sourced from Garrihy's, Doolin

All main courses come with a side plate of vegtables and potatoes

SWEET MENU

Sticky Toffee Pudding
Served with Butterscotch Sauce and Vanilla Ice Cream
€7.80

Lemon Posset
A Light Cooked Lemon Cream, Shortbread Biscuits and
Raspberry Sorbet
€7.80

Dark Chocolate Delice

Served with Vanilla Ice Cream

€7.80

Freshly brewed tea or coffee served with Petit Fours
Decaffeinated tea, herbal tea, and decaffeinated coffee
€3.30 per person

Dessert Wine: Muscat de Beames de Venise

1\2 Bottle €24.00

Glass €8.50

Irish Coffee €7.50

ENJOY!

Chapter 14

GALWAY

Doors Open to Explore

Were you hoping to find friendly leprechauns on your visit to Ireland? Doug and I didn't spot any live ones but we found plenty of friendly people, and you'll find the Irish to be some of the friendliest people in the world! Whether they are blondes, bru-
nettes, or redheads, they're all as kind as you could hope to meet. And guess what? We did find plenty of leprechaun souvenirs—they are all over Ireland, but Galway seems to have more than most places.

In Galway, you will enjoy some of Ireland's most beautiful scenery. You can enjoy sites like the Burren, shopping in the Eyre Square, visiting St. Nicholas' Church, Lynch's Castle, and University College, or seeing the Spanish Arch and O'Brien's Bridge. You can even enjoy a banquet dinner at the famous Dunguaire Castle, built in the 1520s and located in Kinvara (only thirty minutes drive from Galway). And don't forget a very generous offer we acquired just for our readers from Shannon Heritage: visit our website www.ExtraordinaryIreland.com for the details.

Before we explore Galway itself, let me tell you a bit about the Dunguaire Castle. Located on the shores of Galway Bay, Dunguaire Castle is probably the most famous landmark in Kinvara. This facility is open daily for visitors from April through October, 10 a.m. to 5 p.m. Although you do not need reservations to visit the castle, I strongly recommend you make them if you plan to take part in a banquet since they are very popular. We found them sold out months in advance! These banquets are held at 5:30 and 8:45 each evening from mid-April to mid-October. You cannot get in without reservations here. You will find the best rates when you call 1-800-269811 or online at www.shannonheritage.com.

Now on to Galway. Galway is a town you can easily use for a base location while you take daytrips in all directions. Train, air, and ferry transportation are all available there, or you can rent a car for your pleasure. We certainly, for great reasons, recommend air travel to reach the Aran Islands!

Galway is located on the western seaboard and is the capital and largest city in County Connaught. It has a strong economy with manufacturing, retail, education, tourism, and services, including health care, professional, financial, and construction. It's said that tourism is extremely important as an economic booster in Galway and that it has been known to bring in as much as €400 million in a year. That is a lot of tourism!

You can immerse yourself in the history and beauty of this area. The city was founded on the east bank of the River Corrib in the late twelfth century by an Anglo-Norman family named de Burgo, who brought many Welsh and Norman merchants. They enclosed the city with defensive walls. The fourteen families who controlled this city were known as the "tribes" and they developed strong trade with the French, the West Indies, and the Spanish. Later, it has been said that Columbus stopped here on his journey of discovery to America, although it appears he was actually on an earlier voyage in 1477 to Iceland.

In Galway again, you can experience all four seasons in the same day. The year-round weather experience is influenced by winds off the North Atlantic as is much of Ireland. Measured rainfall is about 45.2" a year, which is not bad compared to our own hometown, and the temperatures remain mild year round. We saw the sunshine, but rarely did we move about without sweaters! It seems that summer temperatures hover around 61 degrees, while winter temperatures are around 44 degrees. Galway's population of approximately 73,000 makes it one of the largest cities in Ireland.

Eyre Square (pictured at the beginning of this chapter) was a favorite place for me because we found many treasures, including my new wedding band, the Claddagh ring. Eyre Square is located in the center of the city and we could see it from our window in the Hotel Meyrick.

This city is a vibrant, alive, and welcoming place where all walks of life can be found. In Eyre Square, it seems as though you can walk forever and shop that way too! Finds from groceries to diamonds and woolen hand crafts appear every few doors. Designer clothing, shoes, and more are easily found, as well as extra luggage to haul your newly purchased treasures home. By the time we were ready to leave Galway, we had left our share of currency behind and we were forced to purchase two more suitcases to bring everything home! Oh, did I mention that you can find pubs behind the doors that are not shopping meccas?

Galway is a magnet attracting artists and writers alike, as well as festivals and parades.

From our hotel room, we watched a music festival that carried us away as we danced merrily around our room and sang along to Frank Sinatra songs and music from so many other eras.

Traditional music abounds in the pubs found almost anywhere in Galway, but you do not have to roam far away from Eyre Square to find entertainment of every kind. Again in Galway we found the pubs had enjoyable entertainment and wholesome to gourmet meals, all at affordable prices, and where one could be casually dressed any day of the week.

Galway also offers art shows, air shows, the Festival of Literature, music and garden festivals, and sporting events. This area is alive most of the year with activities, so if you are looking for a festival or similar activity, Galway is probably a city you want to explore and use as a base camp!

We love Galway and will be back!

HOTEL MEYRICK

A World of Luxury

When I first began planning our surprise trip to Ireland, I found three people whom I depended on the most. They were representatives of the Fitzwilliam Hotel, Loch Lein Country House Hotel, and Hotel Meyrick. I first met Aoife Macken through the Hotel Meyrick website. Aoife provided me with so much information about the history of this fine hotel that I was sure we would enjoy our stay. I do not know how you feel about the locations you want to visit, but we wanted to know everything we could,

Meet Aoife Macken

especially when visiting historic locations. So I hope you will enjoy and find helpful the following information as you plan your trip to Ireland!

The Hotel Meyrick first opened its doors to the public in 1852. It was originally known as the Railway Hotel. The Meyrick/ Railway was built of limestone ashlars at a cost of 30,000 pounds, and that was over 160 years ago! One of the original pieces that still remains today is the fireplace dating back to 1845.

On October 19, 1855, Lord and Lady Clanricarde hosted a ball at the Meyrick/Railway for all military ranks from Galway, Mayo, Clare, and King's County in celebration of the Galway Militia parade in Eyre Square,

Denise Horan, Reception Manager

celebrating the presentation of the colors by the Marchioness of Clanricarde. For many years it was said to be the most successful ball ever held in Galway!

The Meyrick/Railway even had a visit from Prince Louis Napoleon of France in 1857. I can hardly believe we stayed in a hotel with such a grand history, yet you will never get the feeling that you are any less important than any other visitor.

The Hotel Meyrick saw hard times during the Irish War of Independence. In 1918, the hotel was taken by the British Army and given back after a treaty in 1922. But that same year, the hotel was occupied by Republican forces that were later forced out only to be replaced by Free State Troops. Finally, following the Civil War, it became a business again!

On June 15, 1919, a reception and dinner was held for John Alcock and Arthur Whitten Brown who completed the first non-stop transatlantic flight. The event was attended by some of the most important dignitaries in the Clifden area.

The Hotel's name was changed to the Great Southern Hotel in 1925. The list of important visitors goes on from here, including October 23, 1933, when the Lindberghs stayed in the hotel after Lindbergh's seaplane landed on nearby Mutton Island as part of an aerial survey by Pan Am.

In 1946, Galway saw a boom in business again and the hotel fell under the ownership of a company named CIE (a company formed after the merger of several railways).

Aoife Macken provided some amazing guest names. We were so surprised by how many famous people had stayed here that we have to list them. Actors who have visited the hotel include Siobhan McKenna, Ray McNally, Rex Harrison, David Hemmings, Bing Crosby and his wife Kathryn, Micheal Mac Liammoir, Hilton Edwards, Gabriel Byrne, John Ford, David Lean, Richard Harris, Fred Astaire, Jack Nicholson, Anjelica Huston, John Huston, Paul Newman (MacKintosh Man), John Wayne, Maureen O'Hara, Victor McLagan, and Barry Fitzgerald.

It makes my heart skip a beat when I think of some of these people whom I have loved and admired. To think we were at a hotel with the best of them is simply amazing!

In addition, several famous writers have stayed here including John B. Keane, Brendan Behan, and Liam O'Flaherty. Liam O'Flaherty stayed at the hotel over long periods during the late 1940s. He was extremely friendly with Tom Flanagan, who supplied him with pots of coffee well into the night as he worked on his books. In fact, one of his books was actually written in the hotel. The old O'Flaherty's Bar in the basement of the hotel was named after him.

To think that I was writing my book in the same hotel as some of the finest people sent chills up my spine—maybe some of this talent will rub off!

Now moving into modern times, in 2006 the Great Southern Hotels group was sold off to the Monogram Hotel group. Hotel Meyrick emerged with a new name and a magnificent and exquisite refurbishment.

In my correspondence with Aoife, I asked her many questions, including places to visit, sites to see, and somewhere we could celebrate our anniversary. She gave us grand advice about places to visit, which we happily followed as a starting place for our exploration. So, let us tell you that if you want to take a walk through Eyre Square, start your morning out at the Griffen's Bakery on Shop Street. For lunch, stop in at a pub for sandwiches, or to enjoy a drink. Then return to Meyrick's Hotel for dinner, or find another pub where you can enjoy dinner with live traditional music to while away the evening!

We have told you about the hotel's history, and I am sure you can find more, but we also want to tell you about our visit. Aoife Macken was one very compassionate woman with a staff almost as great. (It would be difficult to beat the efforts she made to provide us with help and information.) Our room the first night was brightly decorated with soft colors. I say our first night since we decided to stay for three nights, although we had expected to stay only two.

Due to an upset in Doolin at the Ballinalacken Castle Hotel, we checked out early and phoned to see if the Hotel Meyrick could put us up, and they, luckily, had one room left. It was not the one we had reserved for the following two nights, but we were glad to take it. If we ever felt as though the world was at our feet, we felt it at the Meyrick.

I wonder whether we will ever again stay in that wonderful first room we experienced. Perhaps when we return, we will draw that same room. Our memories of it are so happy; life seemed to turn around for us in this magical place where we had no worries for the first time in years. I did not need a Castle stay any longer—and now I was no longer sad because we did not get one!

Guys, if you want to sweep your woman off her feet, this is the place! And all of you who are single, go for it! We celebrated our anniversary all over Ireland, but three locations were extra special—Dublin, Fossa, and the Hotel Meyrick in Galway!

The room we were moved to the

Celebrating Our Anniversary Once More in Ireland

next morning was exceptional. Words are going to be difficult to find to explain it, so we'll let the photos do most of the talking.

We can tell you when we entered the room, there was a seating area straight ahead of us. A bathroom large enough for a very large bath and shower and double sink was on the right, an enormous vanity and a large double door closet were outside the bathroom, and a king-sized bed was in an alcove type area, with window views of Kennedy Park and the city.

From our windows we were able to take photographs of the park

and of the bicyclists as they re-turned to the finish line in a race for a cancer fundraiser.

All around, the Hotel Meyrick was a fabulous experience we will never forget.

THOMAS DILLON JEWELERS

Restored Faith in Humanity

Thomas Dillon Jewelers has been described as "the smallest museum in Europe with the biggest gift shop."

It proudly houses some of the very first Claddagh rings made between 1700-1800 by Gold-smiths Nicholas Burge, Richard Joyce, and George Robinson. It also displays the "world's small-est Claddagh ring" which fits on the top of a tailor's pin. Other exhibits include examples of rings at various stages of production, from wax blanks to the Thomas Dillon Jewelers finished product and a selection of tools used during the process.

This small but quaint jewelry store sits among what appear to be giants in the fashion industry, but it is itself the giant! This little store is where the history of Claddagh Gold began—the ring with so many hundreds of years of history.

After reading about the meaning of the Claddagh ring, I remembered see-ing my grandmother's as a child. I decided I would like to have one of my own as an anniversary ring, especially since we were in the midst of plan-ning our trip to Ireland. We searched online prior to traveling to Ireland, and because I was afraid that the rings would be difficult to find, I was determined to find the source of the original design and order a ring for the day we repeated our vows!

To our surprise, the Claddagh ring is in every store all over the country, or so it seemed! But most were embellished with trappings we were not interested in. We only wanted the plain gold band with the Claddagh design cast onto the ring. I made the mistake of ordering the ring at what we believed was the jewelers who had pioneered the design. (I ordered with the understanding that if we did not like it, we did not have to buy it.) When we discovered that these were not the original jewelers, we bought other items, but not our band. Discouraged, we walked around only accidentally to stumble into the very small store that had what we sought. WOW! Faith had been restored. This was the original jeweler, and we were so excited when we found the perfect anniversary band.

Have you ever seen or heard of a Claddagh ring? It's a ring that represents love, so I would like to tell you about it as an old Irish tradition.

The Claddagh features two hands clasping a heart, and usually surmounted by a crown in the distinguishing design.

The symbols are said to be as follows:

> Heart—represents LOVE
>
> Crown—represents LOYALTY
>
> Hands—represent FRIENDSHIP

These rings are worn in three different ways with the meaning depending on the wearer, and in cases of a gift, the giver. They may be worn to represent engagement, marriage, eternity, or friendship.

If you should observe someone wearing this ring, you may tell the status of that person by the way the ring is being worn.

If worn on the right ring finger, the heart pointing to the fingertip, then that person is free of commitment.

With the ring turned around, and worn on the same finger, it usually signifies the wearer is romantically involved.

When the ring is worn on the left hand, on the wedding finger, it means the person is engaged or married.

Here again is another example of the Claddagh ring only in a wedding band. This style is popular for both casual and formal weddings. We decided to buy this one for the special day when we would repeat our vows to each other after twenty-three years of marriage (twenty-five from when we first met), rather than to wait for our Silver Anniversary.

We were on the trip of a lifetime and wanted to make the most of it, celebrating for three weeks instead of only one day! After all, in reaffirming our love, why not do so in a way that allowed each day of our celebration to be another special memory?

No matter how long you are married, romance should still be alive; you just need to keep the fire burning!

KYLEMORE ABBEY

Now, wouldn't you love to live here? I'm sure a full staff would be needed to keep it up, but if you could afford to own this place, the staff would probably not be an issue! You do feel wrapped in luxury during the tour of Kylemore Abbey, and with a little imagination, you can be transported to another era.

Kylemore Abbey offers visitors treasures to view and a chance to understand the struggle of the nuns and all they endured to create this self-sustaining environment and the life they made here.

This absolutely stunning architectural masterpiece, located in the heart of Connemara, is on the banks of Lough Pollacappul at the base of the Druchruach Mountains. It is a warm and peaceful landscape. It's no wonder this is the most popular Abbey in Ireland.

The Abbey has many sites of interest. You can take a tour of the main building and see some of its history. The Gothic church, set on the grounds of the Abbey, is the jewel in Kylemore's crown and has been lovingly restored.

Besides touring the buildings, you may also enjoy walks around the estate to see the various gardens where they raise their own food, or stroll through the walled Victorian gardens. We found some great ideas here on how to collect rainwater for gardens and to contain the water you use in your garden so it will not just run away but stay in the areas needing the water the most.

History of Kylemore Castle

Your visit would not be complete without seeing and hearing Kylemore's enchanting history as interpreted in detail, room by room.

Kylemore Abbey's Gardens

The Abbey was originally built by Mitchell Henry, M.P. in 1864 (he was a native of Manchester city), and it took him four years to complete this gift for his wife. When first constructed, it was called Kylemore Castle and was the personal home of Mitchell and Margaret Henry.

Connemara was a popular destination for fishing and hunting before the Henrys arrived in the area. Henry Mitchell often visited during fishing season. Tradition has it Mitchell and Margaret visited Connemara and rented the Kylemore Lodge. They fell in love with the beauty all around, so they dreamed of someday building a home there. The Kylemore Lodge was the original building on this site where their dream did come true and where Kylemore Castle was built. (Now, I am a sucker for romance so this story really touched my heart!)

Mitchell's father was a cotton merchant who was of considerable means, and upon his death, a considerable inheritance was left to Mitchell. From those proceeds he purchased Kylemore Lodge and built this glorious, majestic Castle fit for royalty. Mitchell built or preserved many amazing features, including gardens, walks, and woodlands, on this thirteen thousand acre estate. The renovations cost a bit more than eighteen thousand pounds. That would be about $29,000, in nineteenth century dollars.

Mitchell encouraged his tenants to join him in reclaiming this marsh land, and forty years later, with his guiding hand, thousands of acres of marsh land was turned into the productive Kylemore Estate. He developed this estate as a political and commercial experiment and the results brought both social and material benefits to the entire region, leaving an impression on the landscape that will last forever.

Mitchell Henry was a loved man and reached out to people during the time of recovery following the Great Irish Famine, by providing work, shelter, and a school for the workers' children. He went on to represent Galway in the House of Commons for fourteen years, but tragedy struck with the death of his wife in 1874, and later of his daughter. After the passing of his wife and daughter, Mitchell devoted himself to his tenants and serving the people of Ireland. He lived in the castle until 1903, before selling it to the Duke and Duchess of Manchester.

How Kylemore Castle Became Kylemore Abbey

In 1920, Benedictine Nuns bought Kylemore Castle, along with 10,000 acres, for a little over £45,000. Some of the lands were later purchased by the Land Commission and divided out among the tenants. The Castle was converted into an Abbey.

Today, Kylemore Abbey is the oldest Benedictine Abbey in Ireland, and its origins date back nearly three-hundred and forty years to when the abbey was first founded in 1665 in Ypres, Belgium. Although in Belgium, that original abbey became the property of Ireland in 1682. In 1688, King James II requested the nuns move to Dublin. However, they returned to Ypres in 1690 after James was defeated at the Battle of Boyne.

The original purpose of the abbey at Ypres was to provide education and a religious community for Irish women during the Catholic persecution in Ireland. Over the next centuries, the Ypres abbey attracted students and postulants from among the daughters of Irish nobility.

The Community had to leave its abbey in Ypres when it was destroyed in the early days of World War I. After running a boarding school for 250 years, this had to be frustrating for them, but they prevailed by continuing despite their plight. They first took refuge in England and later in County Wexford, before eventually settling in Kylemore in December 1920. At Kylemore, the nuns opened an international boarding school and established a day school for local girls, which still remains today. The nuns were hardworking and ambitious, operating a farm and a guesthouse, while managing several other projects.

To recap briefly, this property houses Benedictine Nuns, a boarding school, a large variety of birds and animals, it offers magnificent surroundings of mountains, woodlands, lakes and rivers, several splendid gardens, the tranquil site of Kylemore Abbey, period furnishings and more than you would ever believe could exist on one property.

Doug at a wooden picnic table specially designed for the Abbey. Now wouldn't this be fun to own!

Although the guest house, destroyed in a fire in 1959, was never reopened, the romantic setting of Kylemore Abbey has continued to attract visitors to its door. Over the years, the nuns graciously opened the estate to the education and enjoyment of all who visit, developing excellent facilities as well as restoring and conserving the many historical features. However, a part of the Abbey is restricted so the sisters can devote their lives to prayer and work.

The Benedictine Community has released a new book *A Light to the World— Reflections from Kylemore Abbey*, which is described as follows: "This book of prayers comes from the heart of the beautiful Connemara Countryside, and reflects the prayers of the nuns throughout the year. As they follow the unfolding liturgical cycle, parallel to the seasons, evocative photographs from the grounds of the Abbey lead you into meditation and prayer. A selection of psalms from the nuns' daily office offers words with which the reader can reach out to the Creator, responding to the stirrings in the soul inspired by personally experiencing natural beauty, life and human endeavor." The book is available in the Kylemore Abbey gift shop for €9.95 ($15 US).

Once again, let me encourage you while you visit Kylemore Abbey to allow yourself to feel the surroundings you are in and be taken back in time; you too will be embraced by both the struggles and the sheer joy the Mitchells and Benedictine Nuns experienced in this incredible Castle story!

Be sure to visit the visitor center and the exhibition housed in the main reception room of the house. If you want to take home any reminders, please be sure to browse their craft (gift) shop which is modest in size but offers a wonderful selection at prices in keeping with many budgets.

There are facilities for the handicapped and a fine restaurant. You will not have to worry about parking or even tour bus parking. The Abbey, its visitor center and exhibition, Gothic Church, and craft shop are open all year. From November to February, the Abbey's hours are 10 a.m. to 4:30 p.m., and 9 a.m. to 7 p.m. the remainder of the year. Good news—it's only a one hour drive from Galway and bus service is available. We did not eat at the Abbey because there was a long line, but we were told the food was outstanding. If you want to enjoy a meal here, make a reservation either before you go, or after you arrive. That way you can go see the sites and return about two hours later and have your lunch or an early dinner.

The information above was found on the Kylemore Abbey website, or taken from our own experience. Some people told us the Abbey was too commercial to visit. But of all the commercial or touristy sites we visited in Ireland, this is one of the few that would have been a tragedy to miss. It is an experience you will not soon forget. We recommend you plan on a four-hour or all day visit here.

Thank you to the Benedictine Nuns and Kylemore Abbey for sharing their interesting history and for giving us such wonderful memories!

The following is a schedule and information provided to me by the Abbey for our book.

FACT & INFORMATION SHEET 2011/12 with RATES

Kylemore Abbey is the number one visitor attraction in the West of Ireland and a "must see" visit for any tour of Ireland.

Set in the dramatic Connemara landscape of mountains and lakes, Kylemore is an iconic attraction, famous around the world. From its beginnings as a romantic gift in the 1860s to becoming home to the Benedictine Nuns in 1920, Kylemore is steeped in history and tales of tragedy, romance, royal visits, spirituality and education. The Benedictine community welcomes visitors to experience the Victorian atmosphere of the restored rooms of the abbey and gothic church and to explore the magical Victorian Walled Garden, nature trails and woodland walks and much more.

Address	Kylemore, Connemara, Co. Galway, Ireland
Phone	+353 95 52001
Fax	+353 95 52037
Email	info@kylemoreabbeytourism.ie
Website	www.kylemoreabbeytourism.ie
Public Entrance Fees	Adult: €12.50*, Senior: €10.00**, Student: €8.50***. FREE Entry for accompanied children aged 10 years and under. Family Type 1: (2 Adults + 1-6 Children/ Student aged 0-17): €33.50, Family Type 2: (2 Adults + 1-6 Children aged 10 years and under): €25. Group rate 10+: €8.00. *Adult aged 18-64 years. **Seniors aged 65 and over. ***Student aged 11 – 17 and students with valid student I.D. card aged 18 and over.
Location	Kylemore Abbey is located in Connemara, Co. Galway, West of Ireland. Located on the N59 between Clifden and Westport, it is easily assessible from Shannon, Galway City, Clifden, Cong and Westport

Directions From Galway City	80Km. Driving Time 1hr. 10mins. Take the N59 for Clifden and continue through Oughterard and Maam Cross until you pass through Recess. Turn right on the R344 signposted Letterfrack, through the Inagh Valley, turn left on to the N59 loop for Kylemore and follow the road.
Directions from Clifden	20km. Driving Time 25 mins. Take the N59 for Westport and continue past the entrance to Connemara National Park, through Letterfrack village and Kylemore Abbey will be on your left hand side.
Directions from Westport	50km. Driving Time 50 mins. Take the N59 for Clifden. You will pass through Leenaun and then Killary Harbour before winding along Kylemore Lake and Kylemore Abbey will be on your right hand side. (Alternate route possible via Croagh Patrick and Louisburgh).
Season	All year.
Dates of Non-Operation	Closed for Christmas. 2011 Christmas closure dates: 19th December to 26th December inclusive.
Opening Times	Open 7 days a week, all year. March-November 9:30 to 5:30 p.m. November-March 10:00 to 4:30 p.m. July & August 9:00 to 7:00 p.m. Bank Holidays will operate as normal working hours.
Groups	Advance booking advised, Contact: Kylemore Abbey e: bookings@kylemoreabbeytourism.ie t: +353 95 52001 Bookings/Visitor Centre Manager: Isabelle Pitorre
Average Visit Length	90- 180 minutes. Allow a minimum of 90 minutes to visit the "must see" attractions of the estate including restored rooms of the Abbey, Gothic Church and Victorian Walled Garden. Visitors are welcome to walk to the Victorian Walled Garden from the Abbey which takes approx. 20 minutes; alternatively, there is a complimentary shuttle bus running every 15 minutes between the visitor centre and walled garden.

Guided Tours of Abbey	From May to September there are complimentary Guided Tours of the Abbey running daily every hour on the hour between 11:00 a.m. to 4:00 p.m. Duration of tour: 20 minutes.
Guided Tours of Walled Garden	From May to September there are complimentary Guided Tours of walled garden at 2:30 p.m. Duration of tour: 25-30 minutes.
Self-Guided Tours	Printed guides & maps available in English, French, German, Spanish & Italian.
Audio Visual	Running daily in English, French & German.
Attractions	1000 acre estate. Miles of mature woodland and lakeshore walks, Nature & Tree TrailsChildren's Play TrailRestored Rooms of the AbbeyMiniature Gothic Cathedral (with lunch time performances during summer months & on selected dates throughout the year). Please see our website for upcoming events & choral performances. http://www.kylemoreabbeytourism.ie/church-eventsAward Winning 6 acre Victorian Walled GardenRestored Head Gardener's House & Garden Boys' House (Bothy) Restored Tool Shed with original gardening toolsRestored Glass HousesOak Plantation, Wild Garden Walk Guided Mountain Hikes (during summer months, booking advised, additional fee applies) On-site pottery studio. Kylemore handmade products available for purchase.

Chapter 15

LIMERICK

Our Final Destination

Limerick is a rapidly growing city with a population of over 90,000 people according to a 2006 census. Limerick, in the Shannon region of Ireland, has much to offer in the way of historical sites and cultural events. Transportation options include bus, rail, auto, and an airport in Shannon, just over twelve miles from the city center.

We did not spend much time here or in any large city except Dublin, where we spent four days. We spent most of our time in Limerick with Anne of Aine Knitwear and our last night celebrating our trip at Bunratty Castle with its Medieval Banquet. Still, Limerick was a great location for us because we were able to fly out of Shannon. I'm sorry that I can't tell you more about Limerick from a personal perspective, but because we studied each area prior to our trip, I will share what we learned.

Not all that long ago, Limerick's economy was driven by meat processing, flour, confectionery production, and a Dell manufacturing plant. The plant employed more than 1,000 people and produced 30,000-60,000 units per day. Dell closed the plant in 2009, moving operations to Poland. I imagine the plant closing was very hard on the local economy.

The University of Limerick, according to what we have learned, is still thriving and well-attended, offering a range of courses including doctorate degrees.

Limerick's history dates back to 812 AD. However, what is purported to be the earliest map of Ireland indicates Limerick may have been established as early as 115 AD, but it is also said that the Vikings destroyed public records so I cannot find additional proof of the 115 AD claim. The presence of the Vikings and Normans is a fact that can be further traced. The name, Limerick, dates back to 561 AD.

The confirmed history of Limerick reaches back to 812 AD when Vikings built a walled city on King's Island. Jumping way ahead in time, a castle under the direction of King John was constructed in 1200 AD, and was taken on three different occasions in the seventeenth century, leading to the Treaty of Limerick. At this time Catholic leaders went abroad because repressive penal laws were passed in 1695, banning Catholics from voting, buying freehold land, holding public office, or practicing their religion in public.

Many years later, Ireland faced a century long depression, beginning with the Great Famine and stretching through the Irish War of Independence and the Second World War.

What I do not understand about the potato famine is that while thousands lost their lives to starvation (about 10 percent of the population), food exports continued, with troops protecting produce from the starving, who had little choice but to try stealing it prior to export! Limerick reportedly lost as many as 70,000 souls due to this famine! What a horrible tragedy.

In the late twentieth and earlier twenty-first century, the city enjoyed a well-deserved economic boom, but one has to wonder if the departure of large industries has harmed this city once more.

Limerick is, by any account, one of Ireland's leading tourist destinations, due in part to its proximity to Shannon's international airport. It is only a twenty-minute drive from the airport. Limerick's tourist trade also benefits from the "Street Ambassador" program. The first of its kind in Ireland, the program consists of people who have agreed to help others find their way or give them advice to help make their stay more memorable. We experienced this act of kindness first hand and firmly believe it benefits Limerick's tourist trade.

RADISSON BLU

We spent our last night at the Radisson Blu in Limerick. If you are planning a trip such as the one we took, arriving in Dublin and departing from Shannon, this is a great choice for your last night (or more). If you are more budget minded and want to use this area as a base for traveling east, west, and inland, the Radisson Blu is probably a good choice. It offers many great features, really nice accommodations, and an easy drive to the airport. This hotel has a nice restaurant, ice machines in the hallway (a rarity in Ireland), very comfortable rooms, and employees who will make your stay memorable.

The Radisson Blu's manager, Gary, was a great help. Be sure to say hello to him for us. If Gary is available, he will do everything he can to help you make arrangements for getting around in the area and securing you a great rate.

You can make reservations for your visit to Limerick at the Radisson Blu using the contact information below.

Contact Information:	
Email:	sales.limerick@radissonblu.com, reservations.limerick@ radissonblu.com
Phone:	(+353) 61 456200, Toll Free 00 800 3333 3333
Address:	Ennis Road Limerick Ireland

BUNRATTY CASTLE & FOLK PARK

A Look Into The Past

SHANNON HERITAGE

What an experience! We had no idea what we were going to see the day we traveled to Bunratty.

Bagpiper welcomes guests to Medieval Banquet

The day was so lovely. As we approached the Castle, we just knew this visit was about to become another really special tour that would take us back in time. And indeed it did!

Bunratty Castle and Folk Park is one of Ireland's top destinations. Putting together two distinctive attractions, Bunratty Castle and Folk Park pro-

vides you a view of life in both the fifteenth and nineteenth centuries!

We were lucky to meet a lovely and well-versed woman named Marie Brennan, who gets all the credit for our incredible journey through the past at Bunratty.

What started out as an hour tour took way over two hours, and believe me, we wished we had planned for at least an entire day. There is so much to see. However, we had plans to attend the Medieval Banquet that evening, and we wanted to get some rest before embarking on that quite spectacular adventure. We knew the evening's festivities would go on for several hours and be a memory that would linger in our hearts and minds forever!

Bunratty offers the visitor two attractions for the price of one and each has a complete set of attributes. Whether you are visiting the Castle and enjoying the fifteenth century, or stepping out into the Folk Park to visit the nineteenth century, you will not be disappointed.

While the Castle, built in 1425, and restored in 1954, offers the visitor a glimpse into the fifteenth and sixteenth centuries with grand furnishings, well known works of art, and tapestries, the Folk Park gives us a true vision of the cottages and houses of the nineteenth century, clustered as they were then at the base of the massive walls surrounding the castle. Leaving the castle and all its medieval furnishings, the finest in all of Ireland according to sources, the Folk Park spreads out in front of you—a peaceful landscape, once stained with the blood so many shed in battle during the many battles fought over it throughout history. These two attractions surely capture the feeling of medieval times.

In researching Bunratty Castle, we found it was originally built in 1277 by Sir Thomas de Clare, and the town came soon after, developing around the castle. However, the property that it is situated on dates back to 970 AD, when it was a Viking Trading Camp.

Reviewing the history of this land and its ownership, you can't help but wonder what life must have been like in the days of yesteryear. Reading the history of the union between the property and the castle built on it, and the diverse owners, you can't help but imagine yourself in those times, wondering, perhaps, whether back then you would have been royalty, surrounded by splendor, or you would have lived a peasant's life, serving the heads of power. I myself, when wandering though the grounds, was in awe of what once was.

Today, the quiet village of Bunratty, with its surrounding countryside, is built upon what was once the thriving town of Bunratty. Shannon Heritage has gone to great care and expense to show you a replica of what once was.

Bunratty Castle is considered one of the finest tower houses still standing in Ireland. The Great Earl of Thomond saw to it, making sure his manor reflected his position of power and wealth—superior to those around him. Today, you see little evidence of the death and murder that followed in the battles fought on these grounds, which we will tell you about shortly. All you see is a tranquil town and the history of its people.

The entrance to Bunratty is as impressive as any. You will approach a section of ancient paved road, see the remains of a moat that once surrounded the Castle, enter a door that leads into the courtyard, and then climb steps to the drawbridge. Once you enter the village, you will see buildings and surroundings from the late nineteenth century, a time when the towns greatly influenced the outlying areas. During that same time, as science evolved to produce modern conveniences, electricity and telephones were mostly for the government and big business, not the general population, so changes were not yet found in the lives of those who populated the countryside.

Life in Bunratty: Can you imagine what the life of an average Irish family would have been like in 1900? Could you live the life they did with no electricity, indoor plumbing, or the conveniences of modern day kitchens?

In Bunratty Folk Park, you will have the opportunity to see how they once lived and sample their daily bread, cooked before your eyes over an open fire fueled by peat!

You may romanticize about times long past, or dread them, but when you see the difference that money made in people's lives back then, you will soon realize it is not much different from today, with one exception—with our modern conveniences, our living standards are better and our lives much easier! Don't miss out on one of Ireland's most authentic opportunities to visit the past with its village life so accurately portrayed.

Some of the information written above was
fuelled by the materials provided to us by
Bunratty Castle and Folk Park. In fact, may
we suggest you visit the gift store there and
bring home your own copy of *Bunratty Castle and Folk Park Guide Book.*

Just to give you a glance at some of the
Castle and Park's history, we have gathered
some highlights for your pleasure.

Bunratty Castle has a violent history and
has been destroyed eight or nine
times. Sources differ on the details of Bunratty's history. For
example, you'll find sources
claiming the son of Sir Thomas
de Clare was killed and the castle
and the surrounding town were
completely destroyed during a
battle between the Irish and the

Normans in 1318. However, other sources claim the daughter-in-law of
Sir Thomas de Clare burned the Castle down, leaving it in ruins when her
husband was killed. So the actual facts are unclear as far as we were able to
determine. Either way, the fact remains, the Castle was destroyed in 1318.

It seems the castle was simply not meant to be in this location, because
after being restored for the King of England, it was once again destroyed in
1332 by Irish chieftains. The castle remained in a state of ruin for twenty-
one years until Sir Thomas Rokeby, Sheriff of Yorkshire, had it rebuilt once
more. But wait! Shortly after its reconstruction, the Irish attacked, taking
Bunratty by force, and it has remained in Irish hands ever since.

In 1425, the McNamara family built the current Bunratty and resided
there until 1475, when it was taken over by the O'Briens of North Mun-

ster. In their efforts to make it a lovely estate, the McNamaras landscaped the grounds with modeled gardens. It was said that at one time over 3,000 deer thrived on this land! Oh what a site that must have been. Sometime later, the O'Briens were given the title of Earls of Thomond, after pledging their loyalty to the King of England. But again, this was short-lived; the end came with the surrender of the castle and grounds to Cromwell's troops and the O'Briens never returned to Bunratty.

The castle passed through many hands and saw many difficulties. By 1804, Bunratty was in a state of disrepair.

Finally in 1954, Lord Gort purchased Bunratty Castle and returned it to all its glory, opening it to the public in 1960.

Rates and Visitor Information

Before you visit, please check Bunratty's website for current rates. The following rates were current at the time of this writing. Be sure also that you enjoy the discount they have extended to our readers. And Enjoy!

Admission Prices:	Adult €9.50, Family €25.00, Child €5.30 in US Dollars; this is converted by multiplying the Euros by 1.5. Example, the adult price of 9.50 Euros would be approximately $15.00. Family rates of 25 Euros would be approximately $38 US with children being slightly more than $8. These US Dollar rates are as of August 2011, so should you need it to be accurate, I suggest you check your bank for current rate exchanges since rates change almost every day.
Opening Times: (As provided by the Internet)	June to August: 9:30 a.m. to 6:30 p.m. (last admission 5.15 p.m.) Closed Good Friday & December 24th, 25th, 26th
Castle:	last admission 4:00 p.m. Year round

Bunratty Castle Banquet	This is an evening of refinement and fun. The entertainment is provided by the Bunratty singers. It includes a four course meal with red and white wine.
	Twice nightly, subject to availability: 5:30 p.m. and 8:45 p.m.
	Adult €45.50, Child (6-9) 50% reduction: €22.75, Child (9-12) 25% reduction: €34.00, Child (0-5): No Charge, Group 20+ 10% reduction: €40.95

Now, two pieces of advice:

One, when you visit Bunratty Castle, be sure you plan on spending the whole day so you can see the entire property. And two, stop by and give the wolf hounds a pet—they are very friendly!

BUNRATTY CASTLE BANQUETS

As for the Banquets, there are two different types to enjoy. The expense is well worth it. You would be hard pressed to find this kind of meal and entertainment anywhere else at these prices. And you get an excellent tour

of the castle. Everyone should visit a castle at least once in his or her life, so go and have a great time. Please tell the staff we sent you and use the discount they have so kindly provided (see our website) so you can enjoy yourself at a reduced rate.

Bunratty offers visitors a traditional medieval banquet and look into Ireland's customs, with dance and laughter filling the barn.

Shannon Heritage's properties in the Shannon Region include the Knappogue Castle,

Harpist at Medieval Banquet

near Quin in County Clare, and Dunguaire Castle located on the shores of Galway Bay, along with Bunratty Castle. All offer medieval banquets, so be sure you don't miss out on one of these experiences of a lifetime!

One thing they all share in common is the welcoming goblet of honey mead!

For forty-eight years, the ladies of the castle, with the help of the Earl's butler, have invited visitors from around the world to dine at the Earl's Banquet at Bunratty. Entertainment is provided by the world famous Bunratty Singers and provides the perfect setting for a mead welcome, four course meal, and good wine.

BUNRATTY FOLK PARK

The Folk Park's story is the beginning of a long train of events that unfolded at Bunratty. We are sure you will enjoy your stroll through the property.

The Bunratty Folk Park, as we said earlier, reflects the life of the nineteenth century. We felt it of interest to tell you how this park came to be and where the first building/home came into play!

With commerce developing and travel on the rise, a jet runway at the Shannon Airport was built in the early 1960s. Sadly, the only way for this to occur was to demolish a farmhouse that blocked its progress. So to preserve this small Irish traditional farmhouse from extinction, the remains were taken to the park and reconstructed, using its original stones and lumber. That farmhouse was the beginning of Bunratty Folk Park only seven miles from its original location.

Three examples of nineteenth century lifestyles may be found at the Folk Park. Over the years, many farmhouses and cottages furnished with original, period furnishings from the turn of the last century were added, representing exact replicas of the traditional farmhouses and cottages from the Shannon Region. This rural lifestyle is representative of rural Ireland in the early 1900s.

The houses give us a cross-section of Irish rural life during the last century: a poor laborer's home, referred to as Gotham Scoir; a small farmhouse representing West Limerick and North Kerry known as The Mountain Farmhouse; and Golden Vale House representing the farmer of means—wealthier farmers would have lived in a home with a parlor and a large, roomy kitchen like this one.

Would you like a preview of what is to come at the Medieval Banquet? If so, then read on. If you want to be surprised, then skip to the next chapter!

We returned to Castle Bunratty on June 20, 2011, at 7:45 p.m., for the banquet that started at 8:45 p.m. We probably did not have to go that early, but it was our last night in Ireland and we wanted to enjoy every moment.

Will you be the one who gets locked in the dungeon? One never knows who it will be unless you attend the Medieval Banquet Dinner!

We want to tell you there will be a lot of people there, so I really do recommend you go early. But not necessarily for seating, as I believe that they pre-assign seats, so they know where to seat you on arrival. You can check this out when you make reservations.

That brings me to one more tip: As soon as you know you are going to Ireland and will be in the Limerick area or the area of one of these castles, make dinner reservations, possibly before you book your hotel. They sell out fast. This dinner is a touristy thing to do, but I plan to do it again. We also plan to return to Limerick so we can attend the Traditional Irish Night, which is entirely different from the Medieval Banquet.

The Medieval Banquet is held in the Castle and is more formal in all regards. You are entertained with music, song, and acting, along with a fine meal. We will not tell you about the surprise you will encounter at the table, but it is fun, and those of you with a sense of humor will enjoy every minute you are there. The meal is fabulous and the wine, called mead, is honey based and so good. Better remember to take some home—it is not easy to find in the U.S.A., but perhaps if you are interested, you might find it at a Renaissance fair or ask your local liquor store if they can order it for you. The honey barrel, which is one way the mead comes packaged, is a great keepsake as well.

The Traditional Irish Night is held in the Corn Barn and is a more relaxed atmosphere, with lively music and traditional dancers. It is said you will find such performers in all parts of Ireland, but we didn't, and it was an event we wanted to see. This alone is a great reason to participate in this Traditional Irish Night.

Ideal situation? Stay in the Limerick area for at least three days. This way you can visit all the sites around Limerick and have two very special evenings at Bunratty. What could be more delightful than taking in one of the evening entertainments each night? The dinner menus are different so it will be a grand treat. If you have two copies of our book, you can present the coupon both times for admission or if allowed, buy all your tickets for both nights at one time!

If you are travelling in southern Ireland, be sure you stop in at Bunratty Castle and Folk Park, in County Clare. It will be the time of your life— filled with memories from the past and new ones just for you! With such an accurate fifteenth and sixteenth century restoration, including Lord Gort's collection of art, tapestries, and furniture, it is the best representation of a complete medieval castle in Ireland!

Contact Information:	
Email:	reservations@shannonheritage.com
Website:	www.shannonregiontourism.ie/25DiscountCard
Phone:	353 61 360788

AINE

A Great Human Interest Story

It was hard to decide what our most exciting discovery was or what to tell you about last, but I decided a heartwarming and personal human interest story should come at the end of this book. It started close to the beginning of our journey and ended in Ireland with this story, but it is really still happening! So here is our own personal adventure, which continues to fill our retirement with excitement!

Amazing, Incredible, Fabulous, Talented, Quiet, Sweet, and Superlative are only a few words I can list to tell you about one of the most exciting parts of our trip to Ireland that made a business venture such an adventure! It was, as I have said, June when we traveled to Ireland, but it was wet and cold enough for hats, mittens, and scarves. These conditions set the stage for getting involved with this INCREDIBLE designer, who would change our lives.

It all started at Blarney Woolen Mills while I was shopping for a hat! I tried on several until I looked around and saw a beret loosely hanging on a hat rack. I took it down and began to feel and act like a little girl playing dress up, but all the while trying to find something stylish to keep my head warm. Well, I found the beret in an ash color and also in indigo blue, but I wanted to be sure I would wear them both before buying the second—I have so many hats at home, all sorts of styles and by different designers, but they just sit and collect dust!

By the next day, my ash-colored beret had been on my head for hours with no major upset to my hair. I convinced Doug to take me back to the Woolen Mills (about an hour's drive each way from where we were staying), so I could buy the indigo blue beret, too. For the next few days, I wore those berets every time I was outside, and I was so happy when I took them off because my hair was never a mess!

The following week, as we traveled the Dingle Peninsula, I was walking down the street when I looked in a window and saw a gorgeous scarf, unlike any I had ever seen before. Amazingly, it looked like it was made of the same yarn as my new berets—and it was the same color!

I rushed in to check it out. Once again I played, trying it on with the beret and loving the look. I even wore it to the counter as I paid. It was an exact match to my beret and had the same designer's name on it. To me that was a sign—it was meant to be. After all, days later and at least one hundred miles away from Blarney Woolen Mills, by sheer accident, just walking down a street, I, by chance, found the matching scarf. It had to be a sign. What else could it be?

Now I was warm—new sweater, new beret, and now a new scarf. This was no ordinary scarf, either.

Aine was the designer's name on the tag for the scarf and the beret. That name would be on my mind for days and in my and Doug's conversations much of the time. It was a name we found ourselves trying to find on the Internet. A name we decided to take home—we only had to find her! I desperately wanted to see what else this CREATIVE designer had to offer! The clerk in the store where I bought the scarf had told me Aine had a website so I might be able to find her that way. For a couple of days, I sent emails to different Anne's online, because the clerk told me Aine's name was spelled Anne and that's how it would be written on  her web page. I should never have believed her name would be different on the website than it was on the tag. I should have listened to that voice in my head called logic!

Of course, the label was going to be correct and the design name and her name would be the same. Once I realized that had to be, I found a designer whose name was spelled Aine. This appeared to be another sign—a fancy spelling for a creative designer! That's not where it ended, however. I needed more than just Aine.

Once I found what looked like the correct listing online, I hurriedly sent her an email about wanting to meet her for my book. I told her I wanted to share her with you, but something else also happened. I asked her whether I could buy the matching scarf for the second beret I had bought. She told me about stores in the area that might have the scarf, but none of them had any left. After seeing her website, I decided to buy as many pieces as possible and bring them home to sell at our Christmas Bazaar. I contacted her again, but it only took a few minutes to realize buying online was not what we wanted to do at all. We decided to meet with Aine so we could interview her for the book and look at her designs. We ended up buying most of what she had with her. In fact, we spent almost every Euro we had in our pockets and still owed her money, which she trusted us to pay when we returned home. Amazing, as I said above. This kind, hard-working woman trusted total strangers to send her money for pieces we were taking with us, people she had never heard of before.

Oh, how I had big ideas! I could hardly wait to get home and finish my book and start ordering more from Aine to take out and sell to retailers. Soon, we worked out an arrangement with Aine to be her Importers/Distributors for the United States. We even had plans to reach out to Canada, as we had met a great Canadian couple, John and Heather, in Ireland, whom we hoped to continue getting to know.

Aine was simply fabulous to us. Talented—yes, that is true also. Aine began knitting at the age of four and, although she will not tell me her age, I suspect that was at least twenty-five years ago. Sorry, Aine, if you are younger, but with these lovely pieces, you have to have been working at your craft for at least that long.

Much of what Aine creates today she learned from her grandmother. And Aine tells us her mother gave her the interest she carried in her heart and mind, leading her to the Limerick School of Art and Design, where she spent the next three years learning to make patterns, the art of design, sewing, and knitting, only this time in a school environment. She then spent another two years doing Computer Aided Design (CAD) and Computer Aided Manufacturing (CAM), working in the industry.

As a girl, she had helped her mother make all their own clothes and helped make hand knit Aran sweaters for a company in Limerick, the city where she was born and raised. She now resides in County Clare in a small area close to Limerick, which she describes as being peaceful and quiet, allowing her to create her designs!

Aine currently works in her studio, which is part of her home, and hopes to open her own shop someday with her sister. Now, that will be a challenge unless she finds others to run it for them, as we plan to keep her plenty busy! With only two people working, and her husband helping when they are really busy, she stays so involved that it is difficult for her to take breaks, or get out much. She's so busy that her adoring husband sends her away on holiday to Italy or France out of reach of telephones and computers.

Currently, Aine has two labels—one for adult women and one for young girls. After working for many years in the industry, she struck out on her own, debuting her designs in 2000 at Showcase Ireland to outstanding reviews.

This young, sweet, quiet woman sells her designs in Ireland, England, Scotland, Wales, Germany, Italy, France, Japan, Canada, and now the USA! She takes pleasure in selling to the smaller boutiques and craft shops that do not want mass produced merchandise. When we came into her life, we were so excited about getting her work out to the public. We, too, began with small boutique stores, but plan to seek out the upscale chain stores so people everywhere can feel the softness of her designs and enjoy the quality of her work!

We have only been showing her designs for a few weeks, but already they are bringing the house down with enthusiasm! Recently, in another conversation, we asked Aine how she got her start with retail accounts. Her story is all too familiar. The general public (our customers), with good reason for the most part, wanted to see how long she would stay in business before committing to purchase. We completely understood that reply as we have run into that ourselves. When we have called on stores directly, many have told us that if we are serious and do the Trade Shows, they will buy from us. It is easy to see their point of view, but it is a shame that so few do not stop to think how difficult it is when you are just getting started to manage the horrid cost of doing these shows.

Not only do you have to stop production, but doing these shows is a lot more than just going there. It costs about $2,000 to enter the average Trade Show, and that's only for a small space. Plus you must rent or buy everything inside the booth, travel to get there, and you have the expense of meals and a hotel room. Then you pray that enough customers will come and order from you so you break even! This is a tough world we all live in and people like Aine, with all the talent and dedication she has, have to face this test of time as well. She is not alone, as every designer goes down the same path. Maybe someday these designers will be repaid for their work rather than have to spend so much money just to be seen.

Aine's bags all have names so you can identify with the ones that excite you! Be sure to ask about the new Molly purse, which is much larger.

Our hope is to talk to a large department store like Nordstrom's, Macy's, or Neiman Marcus. But Aine says even if she starts taking large orders, she will take her time and maintain the same quality and attention, without compromising her belief that each piece must be perfect and based upon her standards.

Aine Knitwear can be found on the market with a price range between $50 to $250, depending on the piece. This is a real bargain when you consider the pieces are hand knit, using some of the best yarns to be found, and the style is like nothing you have ever seen!

With the very long hours that Aine works, she has little time for hobbies, so she finds her joy in traveling or visiting her or her husband Steve's family. She also enjoys spoiling her nieces and nephews and, as she says, "being the cool aunt."

Aine not only hand knits her designs, but she also designs and makes her own fabrics from only natural yarns using knitting and felting techniques. She says she also uses a tweed fabric from a local woolen mill about ten miles away from her studio.

She uses hand flat knitting machines and hand cuts, and she hand finishes all her designs from start to finish. "Each piece is made by one person, so each piece is slightly different." This is why we fell so in love with Aine's designs—her commitment to quality.

When I asked Aine whether the flowers she uses on most pieces are a felted process, she said, "Yes, this way we can make sure that all the colors match and have control over the quality of the pieces."

I also asked Aine what was the most exciting thing she had ever done; she replied, "When Steve and I got married, we bought a broken down old farmhouse and spent three years bringing it back to life." I can just imagine how perfect that farmhouse must be considering her design skills.

When you hear her answer to, "What is the most important thing to you about your business?" her reply will make you fall in love with her based on her attitude alone! She told me, "I am very proud that my business is Irish designed and Irish made. In the current 'global market' it seems to me that it is too easy to outsource to cheaper labor markets and tell your customers the product is handmade, when in fact it could be handmade by children in the Third World. I am passionate and determined that my business will not only be environmentally aware through the use of only natural yarns, but will also be ethically aware no matter how my competitors choose to operate."

I also asked Aine, "Do you have any advice for the women whom you design for?"

I was tickled by her answer: "Buy Áine knitwear! Live life to the fullest, smile, and don't be afraid to change things you don't like. Life is too short to hold grudges or hope for change; get out there and do it yourself."

In our many conversations, I asked Aine whether she had thought about a man's design line, and to my pleasant surprise, her reply was that she is in the middle of designing a line for men! She plans to launch it in 2012, at Showcase Ireland, and it will debut in the USA on January 13-17, 2012, at the Seattle Gift Show. So look out women—your men are going to look as handsome as you are stunning in Aine designer Knitwear!

Not many designers can be described as superlative, but Aine fits almost every meaning of the word. Once you have met her through her designs, you will want to know her and her work even more! Be sure to ask for her designs in your favorite upscale boutiques or high end department stores. If you can't find her, just email us at RosemaryAdkins@ExtraordinaryIreland. com and we will help you find a store near you, or help you find what you are looking for!

We hope you have enjoyed reading about this marvelous designer and that viewing the photos and knowing how she began her career peaks your interest to learn more. Traveling is such fun, but when you are able to combine it with experiences like this one, it is such a bonus. Even without the business end, which was a fun story to us, the story behind Aine keeps me wanting to know more about her and her fabulous work. How about you?

As a final note, I would like to tell you that Doug and I grew up in an era where your word was the most precious commodity in life. It said everything about you as a person. We want to go on the record to say we have enjoyed working, laughing, associating, and knowing people with high moral standards, integrity, and, most importantly, sincere honesty. Now we are happy to include Aine among those we most cherish in this way. She has influenced our lives in a positive way with her attitude and ambition. We are most pleased to be her U.S. business associates (importers/distributors) by nothing more than our word! Hers and Ours.

This experience has changed our lives in such a positive way. Doug retired in May, prior to our taking this journey, but then, one month later, he was back at work, helping as not only my partner in life, but also my partner in this new importing adventure. I do hope, while reading this wonderful story about Aine, that you realize the possibilities and new paths that can open up for you when you travel and stay busy. Theory has it that you stay well and happier with a busy mind—in that case, we should have a much happier life since our growing business is keeping us very busy!

I would like to share just one more thing with you. For over twenty years, I have had the pleasure of knowing a special person who has his own business, which I visit every few weeks. His name is Terry Mestrovich of Headlines located in Bremerton, Washington. Terry is very happy that we have found yet another interest in our lives. He has a unique boutique attached to his salon where he sells his very own fine jewelry creations. Terry decided to add Aine's designs to his shop. A fitting location for her designs!

Recently, Terry telephoned to let me know that a very good client from Scotland had been in his shop while in the country. Terry shared Aine's website with this client, who recognized the names of stores that carry Aine's products in her hometown in Scotland; she plans to buy Aine's products once home. This must be what they say is a small world! Terry plans to carry Aine Knitwear in his place of business in both Bremerton and Seattle, Washington.

We do not have a storefront since we are importers who provide these designs to retail stores so our offer to you is a onetime purchase per customer. Visit our website for details. Further purchases can be made through one of our retailers. For a list of those locations, please contact us:

Contact Information:	
Email:	RosemaryAdkins@ExtraordinaryIreland.com
Website:	www.ExtraordinaryIreland.com
Phone:	360-377-9199

Remember these designs are new to the United States, but as 2012 progresses, we hope to have them available nationwide.

Thank you for the opportunity to share our trip to Ireland with you. We wish you all the best should you decide to take a similar journey.

Chapter 16

GOING HOME

The Airport

Our journey home began in celebration the night before at Bunratty Castle with a special last night dinner. The next morning we were ready to begin our long travel home. This day was filled with mixed emotions—sadness for leaving a country we love and where we had found so many memories; happy to be going home to our own wonderful country, family, and to our dog, Sandy, a very sweet chocolate lab.

Little did we know how involved our trip to the airport would be. We first returned our rental car, which was no big deal, and the airport was within minutes of the rental office. But the process of going through the airport was time-consuming, so be sure you give yourself plenty of time.

Sandy

Next, we checked in with our airline at the airport, after which we went upstairs to the gift shop and waiting areas. You can find just about anything you might want to take home at the airport gift shop. There is also a restaurant and the "Tax Back" credit window. You don't want to miss this since there is a 21 percent tax on purchases, but if you present your receipts at the tax back, you get a refund. (Remember, you have to submit your receipts at the airport or you will not be able to get a credit later.)

After you take care of the tax back credit, you need to go through customs. Here you must show your carry on and get screened, providing your passport and whatever information is asked of you, before moving on to the last check in—security check for the airline! We thought we would have a leisurely stroll to the gate, but all of these checks took time so that was not the case. I do recommend that you arrive no less than three hours ahead of your departure time.

Our flight home was so nice. And it was a relief compared to our flight there. We have nothing against children; we love them, but on our flight to Ireland, we had a child of about four across from us who threw tantrums and screamed most of the way! This was a real aggravation, and, of course, the child's parents did nothing to make it behave. I tell you this so you take ear plugs if you want to ensure peace and be able to sleep on the long journey without the possibility of someone screaming in your ears!

Furthermore, we had fought with the airline about our seats on the way to Ireland. Did you know that even though you book a trip for two on an airline, even if you have booked and been given a seat assignment for the two of you, someone can come along and request the seat you are in, and if the airline chooses, they can separate you in order to give that other person the seat they want? It is true. And it is what Continental Airlines did to us on our way to Ireland. I begged, cried, and called everyone we knew for help—not even the home office would help us. I complained bitterly about the way they treated us en route on the biggest vacation of our lives when we got home. The response from the CEO's office was no seat is guaranteed and there is nothing that states traveling companions will get to sit together. So beware! It could happen to you, but at least you know about it now.

On the way home, we were much luckier. We decided to pay to fly First Class, something we had never done before, but it was a great bonus and well worth it for us. The trip was without incident—we were seated together and we had no screamers. The whole trip home was splendid.

I can't say that our arrival was the same. When we went to pick up our luggage at the airport, we found that the two new suitcases we had bought in Ireland had been destroyed—the entire end of the suitcases had been ripped open. There was no one at the airport to whom I could report the damage, so I sent a claim in the next morning, which was ignored. The airline has never paid one dime for anything we lost. I was especially upset because as a secret, I had purchased two hand knit cashmere tweed woollen scarves for my husband to give him for our actual anniversary date after we returned home so once again we could share the moments we had found so special in Ireland. I had also lost some fine linen pillowcases purchased from a specialty store in Kinsale. Remember, I told you I am a romantic at heart and these two pillowcases were with handmade lace trim that made them so soft to the touch—with a romantic and elegant look for the bed. These items were expensive, but more importantly, they came with memories. It's really a sad day when you are careful and yet someone else can steal away precious memories and not even say, "I'm sorry!" They said I had to have reported it at the airport even though there was no one there! The photos I took at the airport did not help either. So again, BEWARE, and find someone, anyone, who can substantiate your claim, because they are not going to believe you once you leave the airport!

FINAL THOUGHTS

Life is too short for allowing memories to fade or escape, so laugh with your partner, love with thought, and forgive without regret. Live each moment as if there were no more, and if you can, forgive those who cause you pain. These are the thoughts and feelings I found exhibited by people in our travels to Ireland. It is a land where so much happened, and yet love and forgiveness are all around you.

The Irish always give a helping hand to hold yours. Wouldn't it be nice if we as a nation held out our hands in friendship, love, and forgiveness too?

Be sure to read the following pages containing travel tips and

Writing Every Possible Moment!

to visit our website at www.ExtraordinaryIreland.com for your special discount offers from the fine people we met in Ireland. We learned a lot on this journey and want to help you avoid our mistakes! We have also included "Fun and Interesting Facts" that we learned along the way. We hope they help you to avoid the unexpected in your travels.

God bless you and yours. Be happy, safe, and have a great time!

Travel Tips

At this point, may I suggest that you consider taking your own tour? Here are some tips to help you in the planning.

INSURANCE AND MEDICAL TIPS

Before you go, be mindful of your health and anything that could go wrong. First, if you cannot budget for the best traveler's insurance, don't go until you can! We tell you this from firsthand experience and out of concern for your well-being—physical, mental, and emotional. We decided to kick off Doug's retirement by meeting our daughter Kecia, and son-in-law, Jonathan, in the Cayman Islands for a week, just two and a half weeks before our three week adventure in Ireland. Midway through our beautiful vacation in the Cayman Islands, I really began to feel bad. Two days later, I was hospitalized with a serious condition. They talked to us about medi-vac possibilities and real trouble. I had had a complete blood test just a month earlier, so this problem was a total surprise. Fortunately for us, we had good health insurance. But we also had taken out traveler's insurance that would bring us home if the condition meant we could not fly safely on our own. It also had a cancellation section that covered us if we had to cut our trip short for any reason. We were lucky and also got great medical care. They got me well enough to travel so I could finish my care state side.

One slight problem—the hospital did not take insurance from out of the country, so be prepared to pay your hospital bill in full before you leave! Call your insurance company and learn the details of out of the country coverage. The insurance company will usually have certain medical facilities you can use, so if you go somewhere not on their list, it can be a problem. You can plan your vacations and do what you want, but please take care of this vital detail to protect yourself and your family or travel companions. Now, I am only sharing this information because I want you to realize the importance of health insurance and especially if traveling out of the country. Then it is truly a MUST!

TOUR TIPS

Planning your own personal tour is a great way to see Ireland and at your own pace. As I told you earlier, we reserved an automobile to rent when we were ready to leave Dublin and see the country. Of course you can do that from any major city where there is a rental agency for vehicles. When we departed Dublin, we got a bit lost due to our GPS not working, but in a way, it allowed us a different, unplanned route to see other areas we found to be amazing. So don't be afraid to explore. You will find your very own treasures where you least expect! Renting a car has its' own advantages, however, driving on the left side of the road can sure send mixed messages from your eyes to your stomach! It is hard to get use to but so worth it. On most of the country roads, riding as a passenger, the lanes were so narrow that at times it felt as though the limbs off the nearby road side hedges could slap you in the face. My husband, as the driver, never had that feeling.

While we were based in Kinsale, we took a very long day trip to Mizen Head. Along the way, we found towns like Skibbereen and Bantry, all offering their own picturesque scenes and interesting shops.

Skibbereen gives you an eerie feeling if you know its history, but nonetheless, it is a quaint area you will enjoy. I say eerie because during the Great Famine, it's reported that this small area lost between 8,000 and 10,000 people to starvation. They were laid to rest in this town.

Bantry, on the other hand, is a small, populated area; its beautiful vegetation and being on the Atlantic Ocean provide a peaceful atmosphere that surrounds you.

On our drive from the Dingle Peninsula, we traveled through Ennis, Lisconnor, Gort, and Kinvarna to mention just a few. In these areas we either explored or just enjoyed the countryside as we traveled to Galway, and we returned via a different route on our way to Shannon and the plane ride home.

Gort was another town hit hard by the Great Famine. It is reported that this small town had a population of approximately 3,600 in 1831. As of five years ago it was only 2,700. After more than one hundred and eighty years have passed, the population has still not returned to what it was. This fact was curious to us, so listening to different people talk about the history while we walked around was interesting. Surprisingly, today, about half of its residents are not Irish but Brazilian, having come to Gort to work in its meat-processing plants.

Ennis, as we understand, was developed in the 1950s to become the Ennis of today. The walking tour in Ennis is said to be one people will enjoy for its history, but we ran out of time and were unable to enjoy this one! If you want to surf the net while in Ennis, this is a friendly town with all the modern capabilities. You can also shop along with the locals on Market Street. So enjoy this town.

Ireland has so much to offer. It is simply difficult to travel more than twenty miles before you find another location that looks too interesting to drive past. This is why we suggest a road trip. One can still enjoy a group tour by organizing a caravan of travelers or taking the tours in various towns you want to explore. And it seems even the smallest towns offer lodgings of some sort.

There are twenty-six counties in Ireland. When you are in Ireland, county names are used very often. For your information, I have listed them here. We strongly recommend you either use our guide with all the information we have provided to explore, or research these counties to see what is there and whether you would like to travel to or through them. Being prepared will enable you to use every precious moment to see and do the things YOU want to do.

Counties are grouped into regions for official statistical purposes: Provided by the Tourist Information Bureau-Ireland

Border—Counties Cavan, Donegal, Leitrim, Louth, Monaghan, Sligo

West—Counties Galway, Mayo, Roscommon

Midland—Counties Laois, Longford, Offaly, Westmeath

Mid-East—Kildare, Meath, Wicklow

Dublin Region—city of Dublin

South-East—Counties Carlow, Kilkenny, South Tipperary, Waterford, Wexford

South-West—Counties Cork, Kerry

Mid-West—Counties Clare, Limerick, North Tipperary

Let me share something with you here that I believe is a common situation with most couples. When my husband and I have gone on vacation without thought or pre-planning and have, in the mornings, asked each other what we would like to do, the conversation goes like this: "Dear, what would you like to do today?" Response, "I don't care; whatever you want to do is okay with me." Sound familiar? We have done that to the point where it would be a few hours of wasted time and nothing was done except asking each other what we should do! Don't fall into this situation, especially if you are on the other side of the world!

HOW AND WHAT TO PACK

Most women seem to over pack! (Sorry, but that is me too!)

We have been brought up to believe we need a purse and shoes for each color we wear—black, navy, brown, and white! Well, I packed just that way, stuffing two suitcases and a carry-on. That meant we had to buy two suitcases to bring home what we bought! I sure did learn my lesson—I was much better than usual, but not at all close to what it should have been. First, take the shoes you find most comfortable to switch off with the ones you travel in and perhaps take along some slippers. Leave the others at home.

Purses—I packed a black and a navy purse and carried a white one! Then I packed a backpack and computer bag for my iPad, and a bag to put them all in! Wow! I hope this does not sound like you.

I carried one purse for two days. I used the white bag for one night. I never used the other two.

I found myself carrying only the backpack and using it as my purse. It was easier. Now, I do not do that at home, but then, I am not moving around and hauling all of them at one time. Take one purse and a backpack! Thank God your male partners do not carry shoes and purses like a woman would—imagine how heavy the luggage would get! And, do not forget the weight restrictions on the airlines—it could get costly.

Some airlines charge for the first checked bags and additional bags are at an even higher charge, so be sure you check on the charges before you book that bargain ticket since it could have a few hidden costs. The only time that may not be an issue is if you travel First Class, but then you could pay extra for luggage and still save a lot of money with regular coach.

Some airlines also limit passengers to a single carry-on bag, which cannot exceed 10kg (22 pounds) in weight. The clue here is to KNOW the facts about all costs before you travel.

CHOOSING LUGGAGE & TRAVELING LIGHT

When packing your suitcases, try to think about who will carry them. Some hotels may not have concierges to help. And remember, if you pack too much, you are just going to have to take it everywhere anyway. Wouldn't it be nicer to buy something extra if you need it than to pack way too much in order to have that something extra you might not use? Like shoes— although I saw some truly nice styles, but I had bought so many, I did not dare buy more shoes!

Also, when selecting luggage, there is a new kind out now that is feather weight with hard sides and wheels that will be the best and will allow you the flexibility you need. Be sure to pack an extra empty suitcase or one that folds up to put inside the main suitcase to allow for the things you will probably want to bring home.

But again, check the policies of your airline for their regulations on what they charge. It could be better for you to ship items home from Ireland and most shops offer that option for you. They also have postal offices in every town.

DRESS CODES IN IRELAND

The only thing we saw was very casual dress like jeans and flats or sneakers for both men and women. We did not see many crop pants for women or shorts for either men or women.

As for anywhere else, if you dine out somewhere nice, dress accordingly—slacks and a dress shirt or sweater for men and possibly a sports jacket; for women a dress or pants suit will be fine. My husband, Doug, took only a few really nice shirts and we bought handmade sweaters he used—that was enough. Jackets were never an issue. Even slacks with a new sweater from Ireland will work for either a man or woman dining out just about anywhere. I found myself wearing my jeans more than most pants—they were warmer and just fine with a dressier sweater.

PACK FOR THE WEATHER!

There is a summer in Ireland, they say, but we were there in June and wore our newly purchased sweaters, hats, and scarves! Remember that old saying—Layer! Take clothes you can layer so if you are cold in the morning, you can easily peel the layers away as you warm up. Winds and rain along the West Coast (Galway down to Dingle and across to Cork) can bring colder weather year round!

If you have ever heard of "sun showers," I really believe whoever thought that expression up was from Ireland! So pack wisely.

If you travel to Ireland in the winter and in some months of the summer, pack a sweater unless you plan on shopping there, which I highly recommend. You'll also need waterproof boots or shoes for walking in the hills or along the water, if you plan to hike. I have mentioned that in June my head was cold, so a hat and scarf would be a good idea, unless, again, you plan to shop! My personal recommendation: Leave the umbrellas at home. They can be bought fairly inexpensively and you can leave them behind if weight issues become a problem. Taking an umbrella could cause more weight in your luggage, which could cost you more than a new umbrella!

Both friends and travel books told me to pack my shorts, but out of three weeks, there was only one day we felt it warm enough to wear shorts.

TAKE CARE OF YOUR FEET

Walking in Ireland can be a strain if you are not used to the cobblestone streets or simply walking a lot, which one will do there. I took three pairs of shoes besides the pair I wore on my feet. That is a bit extreme, but I do recommend two pair, so you can change them every day. I developed what was called a "marathon foot" from walking so much. It is a callus on the end of my big toe! That was from my foot shifting back and forth inside the shoe as a result of too much walking. Wearing open toe shoes in the summer with socks if it is cold is another good idea so you can avoid what happened to me.

PACK THESE FOR SURE!

Adapters and/or converters for any electrical equipment. Electricity in Ireland is supplied at 220 volts AC, which may damage some equipment. We took an adapter for foreign countries that we bought from the AAA Travel stores, but then we also bought a new hair dryer and curling iron in Ireland, which is a better idea if you can find and afford them.

We had to buy batteries for my camera, which are expensive there, so pack what you think you may need along with extra memory cards.

YOUR DOCUMENTS

Pack your documents in a safe pouch like a passport holder. The airline vouchers and passports can easily fit in these and keep them safe. Doug carried one a bit larger that held our confirmations, tickets, emergency contacts, identification, medical cards, and medical history. There is a "tax back" offer in Ireland, but you need to keep track of all your receipts to claim that benefit, so the pouch can be useful for that as well. Or use a separate one for receipts, which is what we did.

MONEY EXCHANGE TIP

It is wise to be sure you exchange at least enough money for tips at the airport, and for the hotel bellman, and taxi drivers. We were sure to travel with several hundred Euros so we did not have to look for cash machines, exchange booths, or worry about banking hours. You may even want to be sure to have enough exchanged to buy refreshments at the airport. Your hotel, in most cases, can prearrange pick up at the airport, but you will find this expensive.

TRANSPORTATION TO AND AROUND IRELAND

Ferry Service

Traveling around a foreign country for the first time can be a daunting task. VisitIreland.com is a helpful resource. We've also compiled a list of international airlines that will carry visitors to the Land of a Hundred Thousand Welcomes, as well as the train, bus, and ferry schedules needed while traveling within the country.

A valid passport is needed to travel from the United States to any European country, but generally, you will not need a Visa in order to visit Ireland. Still, it's best to check before you go.

Arriving by Air

Although the Republic of Ireland has four major airports (Shannon, Dublin, Cork, and Knock) most traffic flows through either Shannon or Dublin. From the Shannon airport you will find bus service to Limerick, and in Dublin, bus service is available to the city center. Both airports' bus services run frequently and offer another option beyond renting an automobile.

The following airlines offer one-stop or nonstop service from the United States:

- American Airlines
- Aer Lingus
- Air France
- BMI
- Continental
- Delta
- US Airways

The following airlines offer one-stop or nonstop services from the United Kingdom:

- Aer Arann
- Aer Lingus
- Air France
- British Airways
- British Midland
- Ryanair
- Virgin Atlantic

Arriving by Sea

Most of the sea arrivals are by ferry to the Republic of Ireland and come into Dublin or DunLoaghaire close to Dublin and public transportation is then available to Dublin.

The same applies in Northern Ireland where public transportation is available. You arrive through Larne Ferryport and transportation is available to Belfast.

Automobile rentals are available at these Ferry Ports and so is a money exchange.

Several ferry services around Ireland connect you to other European areas and to the Aran Islands.

Airline Travel within Ireland

Airlines you can book to travel within the country are:

- Aer Lingus
- Aer Arann
- Ryanair

Please remember to make use of the Tourist Information Centers since most information regarding tours, travel, hotels, B&Bs, restaurants, and more are available there.

Be sure you carry proper identification such as a driver's license and passport with you at all times and keep them safe, especially when crossing the border into Northern Ireland.

RENTING A CAR

Ireland has many automobile rental agencies, so be sure to book ahead of time. Most vehicles are standard transmission, so those are more easily rented than automatics. We rented a small car with an automatic transmission. Because we had no idea that manual (stick shift) was more popular, what we got was a car that was not so great. The body was all scratched up and it did not ride well. Small—to us a small car is large enough for luggage for two—Not So! We had to upgrade so we could get our luggage in the car! So be sure to check the different agencies online to see what they offer. Renting a car in Ireland is not the same as renting a car here. Based on experience and hotel management recommendations, we have found the following companies best. We were happiest with them in this order:

- Sixt
- Argus
- Auto Europe
- Avis

Automobiles are for rent at major airports, large cities, and ferry ports. Be sure the price includes unlimited mileage, collision damage, and VAT (tax). Also be sure you have the proper insurance because we were told your own policy at home will most likely not cover you in Ireland.

When you book online you may be able to see what types of cars are available through each agency. Just remember small in Ireland is really small! These cars are in high demand so be sure you won't be disappointed and book your car right the first time. Think luggage and what will fit in the car and remember some roads are so narrow two cars cannot get passed each other. Small cars, therefore, may be difficult to get in the busy seasons. That is why you book at the time you make airline reservations. We watched many people either book vans and wagons or even a sporty car because they hadn't made reservations far enough in advance.

We did not see many restrictions for drivers as long as they held a current International Driver's license. We found those to be easy to obtain. We just went to AAA Travel office and showed them our current license, filled out the information requested, paid our fee ($20), and we were then issued the International license. We also recommend that if you are traveling with someone, you each have a license so either can drive. Be aware when renting a car, the rate will increase for two drivers. Some companies have an age barrier so be sure to check. There may also be an issue about taking the car to another country or even to Northern Ireland, so be sure to check that as well.

(Being prepared will help you enjoy your trip a whole lot better so please either use our book to help you know what there is to see or do your homework on areas of interest. I have tried to include many sites that are tourist minded with our opinions about their value. They are honest opinions with no obligations owed to anyone.)

Being prepared will also enable you to use every precious moment to see and do the things YOU want to do.

FUN & INTERESTING FACTS

When You Buy An Irish Sweater At Blarney Woollen Mills

Honeycomb

When you buy an Irish sweater it comes wrapped in history
And tied with threads of legend, a Celtic legacy.

On the rugged Aran Isles of Inishmore and Inishmaan
And Inishere — centuries ago — this tradition first began
With early island dwellers who spent remote and frugal days
Recording primitive beauty in stitches that amaze.

The Cable Stitch

An eminent historian claims the task was borne and shared
By women skilled at spinning yarn and men who deftly dared
To cross and twist the thick wool threads, their hands adept with ropes
That they had made, by braiding hemp to moor their fishing boats.

Tree of Life

Together family members in the kitchens of their homes
By light and heat of turf fires using sharpened quills and bones
Knit heavy oiled-wool sweaters tight 'against wind and rain
To embrace their men in loving warmth 'til safe in port again.

Irish Moss Stitch

And these fishing shirts of pale 'Bainin' were embellished with designs
Composed of complex, wondrous stitches that were symbols of their times.

The Trellis stitch for stone-walled fields
The Basket for the cod
The Tree of Life for family strength
The Trinity for God
The Zig-Zag stitch for shoreline cliffs
The Double Zig-Zag for all
The ins and outs of married life
The Cable lest you fall
The Irish Moss for Carrageen
Gathered at low tides
The Diamond and The Honeycomb
For success hard work provides

Diamond Stitch

Basket Stitch

Trellis Stitch

These Traditional Aran Stitches enjoy a beauty all their own
Each family chose a pattern stitch and by this stitch was known.

Thus clothed, fishermen in curraghs rowed the seas of Galway Bay
In search of cod and herring and lobster for their pay.
They gambled with the ocean's moods, knew peaceful-prayerful ride.

Zig-Zag Stitch

When watery beasts claimed men and boat returning them to shore
On the mainland thirty miles away to sail again no more,
The Aran Sweater Family Stitch told the identity of
The fisherman whose kin helped knit his epitaph with love.

...Lest this ancient bond be broken lest the past its story fade
When you wear your Irish sweater, treasure how it first was made
E.A. Manning '94

CLADDAGH RING MYSTERY

There are many stories surrounding the Claddagh Ring, but we know for sure that what it stands for can be summed up as "Let Love and Friendship Rule Forever!"

One story is about a woman named Margaret Joyce who was married to Domingo de Rona, and upon his death she inherited a large sum of money that she used to help many others. As a result, it is said that she was rewarded by a bird flying overhead and dropping the ring in her lap!

It is also said that a young man whose name was Richard Joyce of Galway decided to leave his true love in search of his fortune in the West Indies. While his ship was sailing on the high seas, it was attacked and taken over by pirates, who sold him into slavery to a Moorish goldsmith. Richard later became well-respected for his talent as a designer of fine jewelry, and when King William III found a way to have the slaves freed, the Moor offered his daughter's hand in marriage. But Richard, still longing for his true love, declined and returned to Ireland in search of his only true love. When he found her and learned that she had remained faithful, he proposed marriage to her and designed this special ring in her honor. Now, I really like this legend. Perhaps it is true?

The last version I read was one that sounds real. It is said that the ring's symbols carry meanings that were intended by their designer and that perhaps go back to the Thomas Dillon claim of originality. The symbols represent a Christian version of this legend, which has it that the crowned heart represents God the Father, and the two hands signify Jesus and the Holy Spirit.

It does not matter what is actually true since I am sure this ring has meant many things to many people over the years, but as long as it is given in the name of friendship and love, what else really matters?

IRISH CUISINE

Irish cuisine is still focused around the potatoes served in various ways at most meals. You will find that they use very little seasoning in Ireland except salt and pepper and rarely do you find sauces or gravies. Cheese is of major importance, with over fifty varieties, and it is still sold by cheese mongers. The soups are different from what we know as a soup with chunky pieces of vegetables, but that does not mean they are not in the soup—they are, but most we found were pureed and quite delicious! We ordered a vegetable soup in one location that appeared to be a split pea, but it had many vegetables—again pureed!

As you may imagine, because of the influence of the sea, fish is a major source of protein, as is lamb. And don't forget about cabbage.

Bread served typically is potato bread or brown bread.

Healthier Food: The food in Ireland overall has less sugar and grease than at home. We found less use of salt and sugar even for pastries that were plainer, but very delicious.

The typical Full Irish Breakfast includes:

- Eggs
- Potatoes
- Oatmeal
- Fresh fruit
- Brown bread, scones
- Bacon and Sausage
- Black and White Pudding

Miscellaneous Tips

Bathrooms: There are no protective toilet seat covers anywhere to provide for good hygiene. You may want to take them with you so you can have a clean place to sit.

Beverages: Pepsi products are far and few between and soda is not that big in most stores or restaurants. Ice is not used in beverages unless you ask, and then only small amounts.

Direct Booking: Book directly with hotels instead of your travel agent. One hotel where we stayed didn't think much of booking companies and informed me they had to use them for business—but you should see what you get for a room when you do!

Driving: There are roundabouts everywhere so get use to them. Gas is very expensive and sold by the litre (liter), so unless price does not matter, you may want to consider a smaller car. And they drive on the left side of the road—most of which are very narrow and lined with stone walls or hedgerows so be prepared for that as well. Be sure to help your husband to ask for directions or you may miss a location all together! Sorry, guys.

Electricity: There are no plug outlets for hair dryers or curling irons in any bathrooms. The only bathroom outlet is for European electric shavers. You may want to consider buying a hair dryer and curling iron in Ireland as it uses 220V, 60HZ. Or you definitely need a converter. The converter is necessary for your computers, games, and anything electronic.

GPS Systems: Take your own GPS (we used Garmin) and have the Ireland program loaded (map). Otherwise expect to pay €14 daily, which is $21, just to avoid getting lost! When you hear the words "RECALCULATING," don't throw the GPS through the window—it simply means you made a wrong turn or missed one! Why is it always a woman's voice?

Kitsap Airporter: Never use the Kitsap Airporter for trips. They will not wait for you to use the bathroom for an emergency, but will hold you up to take on extra riders even though they say no delays are allowed. I was told that they would not wait for me to use the toilet even when it was an emergency. For the $36 they charge, you can take a cab or rent a car!

Pudding: It's blood pudding and is part of EVERY Full Irish Breakfast.

Rest Stops: There are none along the roads, so it can be miles before you find a restroom. Pubs and grocery stores are almost always accommodating. We bought many drinks, crackers, and snacks along the way so we could use their toilets without feeling strange.

Tipping: Everywhere you are expected to tip—for parking, bell-persons, at airports, restaurants, etc. So carry lots of small bills or coins. (There are coins for single Euros too.)

Weather for a Summer Adventure

Having said that temperature averages can be tricky, here are a few charts which show the averages for several points around the country. These are thirty-year averages, and the "average wet days" are days with rainfall measures of more than one millimeter.

WESTERN IRELAND (GALWAY AREA)

June: High 61.9 (f)   Low 48.6 (f)   with 10 wet days

July: High 65.3 (f)   Low 52 (f)   with 9 wet days

August: High 64.8 (f)   Low 51.6 f)   with 11 wet days

SOUTHERN IRELAND (CORK AREA)

June: High 63 (f)   Low 49.3 (f)   with 10 wet days

July: High 66 (f)   Low 52.5 (f)   with 9 wet days

August: High 65.5 (f)   Low 52 (f)   with 11 wet days

SOUTHWESTERN IRELAND

June: High 62.6 (f)   Low 47.8 (f) with 12 wet days

July: High: 65.1 (f)   Low 50.4 (f) with 12 wet days

August: High: 64.8 (f)   Low 49.6 (f) with 14 wet days

EASTERN IRELAND: DUBLIN AND COASTLINE

June: High 63 (f)   Low 49.3 (f)   20 Wet Days

July: High: 66 (f)   Low 52.5 (f)   22 Wet Days

August: High: 65.5 (f) Low 52 (f)   22 wet days

Please be aware that while these days have rain, the rain is not always heavy and often just showers. Reported by Wolfram/Alpha & Weather2Travel

NORTHERN IRELAND

Rainfall measurements are reported as follows: June and July are reported to have a precipitation of 60% and August of 80%.

Temperatures: June through August:

63.5 (f) typical day with daylight hours that begin before 5a.m. until 10 p.m.

Emergency Contact Information
for U.S. Visitors to Ireland

American citizens visiting or residing in Ireland should note that the emergency number for the Irish police, rescue, and fire departments is 9-9-9.

If you are an American citizen in Ireland in need of emergency assistance outside of regular business hours (including weekends and holidays), please call the Embassy's main number (01-630-6200) and follow the prompts to reach the operator. You will be connected to the U.S. Marine Security Guard on duty who will assist with directing your call.

If you are an American citizen in Ireland in need of emergency assistance during regular business hours (8:30 a.m.–5:00 p.m.), please call the Embassy main number (01-668-8777), press 1 at the first recorded message, and follow the prompts to reach the American Citizen Services Unit.

The U.S. Department of State has a call center that provides information on worldwide situations that may affect American citizens. The Call Center also provides general information.

Operators are available Monday through Friday from 8:00 a.m. to 8:00 p.m. Eastern time and 24 hours a day during crisis situations.

From overseas: 001-202-501-4444 (Toll call)

In the U.S.: 1-888-407-4747

$AVINGS!
SPECIAL OFFER FOR OUR READERS

Thank you for journeying to Ireland with us through the pages of this book.

If you want to take your own trip to Ireland, be sure to visit our website where we have special offers available for our readers for many of the locations we visited. We will be updating these as new offers become available. You can visit us at:

WWW.EXTRAORDINARYIRELAND.COM

BUNRATTY CASTLE